REDEMPTION...

BOOK 3...

The SEQUEL,

TO MY REAL-LIFE SAGA...

Written By, GERNEL L. DARRELL

GW00809086

...TUB...

Gernel01tub@gmail.com

Written and Published by,

Gernel Leroy Darrell…

ISBN-13: 978-1987433548

ISBN-10: 1987433548

My Books…

Redemption, A Real-Life SAGA, Book 1…

Redemption, Book 2, The SAGA Continues…

(This Book) Redemption, Book 3, The SEQUEL TO My Real-Life SAGA…

These Books and my Future work is also…Available from, Amazon.com, CreateSpace.com, and other retail outlets…

Also available on Kindle and other devices…

i

Dedication Page…

I Dedicate this Book, to All the People that have Crossed Paths with Me, in My Journey of Life…

And who have took the time out and gave their input on My Books, no matter how big or small…

Every piece of a Puzzle, makes it All Complete…

Special Thanks, To My MOM of-course…

And My 2 Lovely Sisters… (CHANTELLE AND SELENA)

Also, Much Love to My 2 Baby Girls FOREVER…

And Finally,

Praises to ME (TUB)…

For Making It All Happen…

THE SEQUEL TO MY REAL-LIFE SAGA...

Table of Context...

REDEMPTION BOOK 3...
The SEQUEL,
To MY REAL-LIFE SAGA...

Introduction...

Welcome to Part 3 of Redemption, A Real-Life Saga...
Which is a True Story of/about My Life... In Part one, I
took you through my life of growing up, and the Detrimental
Mistake that landed me with Life in Prison... In Part 2/
Book 2, I took you through my Crazy emotional roller
coaster of Jail and My Soul Searching, as I looked for an
Answer from GOD as to why I'm in here/in Jail, and also, a
way out of this hell hole of a Jail...

In this Part... Book 3... I was just released from Prison/
Jail, and I'm on Parole for the next 8years... If I Fuck Up,
and get in Any Trouble... I'll be back in Jail, and have to
finish my remainder of time in Jail... And being behind Bars
Again, would Definitely, Kill Me!!!

I worked So Hard to get out of Jail, that I feel, that once
Released from this Place/ Jail... I Need A Nice Long
Vacation!!! And my Vacation Starts, AS SOON AS, I step
Foot out this mother fucking Jail!!! So, I really don't want to
be the productive citizen, I told them I'll be, so they can let
me go... I just wanted Freedom and to be Left Alone, to
find My Own Path...

Travel with me, through my wild journeys, and see if I can
maneuver through the obstacles that present themselves and
Stay out of trouble... I must Defy all Odds, and get Parole,
Over and Done with, without going Back Jail, and also gain
MY Complete Freedom/Victory...

WIN... LOSE... OR DRAW...

I MUST DO IT ALL... MY WAY!!!

REDEMPTION BOOK 3…
THE SEQUEL
TO MY REAL-LIFE
SAGA…

…CHAPTER 1…

…FREEDOM IS PRICELESS…

I was just Released from Westgate Correctional Facility, I have spent the last 5 years in that Damn place, called Prison/ Jail and now it's Finally over!!! Well my time in Jail is done for now, Thank GOD, but I ain't/ am not completely Free yet… I made a deal with the Prison/Court system to be Released on Parole… They basically granted me parole, but I say deal, because I'm got so many Rules and Regulations to follow… But I'll prefer to be free and follow rules then be in that damn place, (JAIL) and getting put in a cell every night… The Prison guard, just walked me to the Gate of the Prison/ Jail compound, and let me Leave/ Walk Free from jail…

I'm on my First Walk of Freedom, since I was 21years old… I wound up in this place for a simple, scenario, that just went bad, and with this Court System, I got dicked/ fucked Bigtime!!! It was no way I was supposed to do any time in jail… Basically this what happened in short… I slapped up some dude, because I would always see him hitting his chick… I just thought it was coward shit, and me who lived in the, "Mind State", that the World was Mine, I decided I was going to discipline him…

So, one night I'm drunk, and I see him... I slap him 3 times, all the while taunting him to fight back... He pulls out a knife and screwdriver and pushes that shit straight in my chest... The screwdriver punctures my right Lung, and the knife stabs me also in the chest, and he drops it... It all happen so quick, all I knew was that I was stabbed, but the shit didn't hurt... So, when he pulls back from stabbing me, he drops the knife... I look down, and when it dropped it landed by my right foot... So, at that instant I dip down and grab the knife, and stab his ass, back in the chest because he just stabbed me in the chest... As I stab him I look up into his eyes... His eyes open wide in shock, and he runs off...

Long story short, I started to, "Die" about 45mins later!!! Like "Really Dying," where the Darkness was coming for Me!!! I Refused, to DIE, and told my boy rush me hospital... That Asshole, (the guy that stabbed me) gets found the next day, Dead... He was found dead with the same screwdriver that he used to stab me in the chest, still in his hand, with my blood on the tip... The police then charge me for Murder... During my trial I don't go on the stand, which I should have... But I listened to my Sell-Out lawyers... In the end, the Jury said Guilty and I walk out of court with a LIFE Sentence!!!

About a Year later, I appeal my case, and they accepted my appeal somewhat, and changed my Murder charge, to Manslaughter, and the LIFE sentence to 12 Years in Prison... Waiting for that appeal was the hardest part of my Life... I was 22 with no chance of getting out of Jail until I was 37 years old... Life is a 25year sentence, in Bermuda... And if you are a really good prisoner, after 15 years, you can get parole... So, with the 12year sentence, I done 4years out of it, and it was do another 4 and be completely free, or since I was a good prisoner, I could take the other option of 8 Years of Parole...

I said Fuck another 4 years in this place, (Prison/Jail) give me parole... A lot of guys say Parole is a trap, because once you take parole, your whole sentence is activated... So, for me the 8 years I have left becomes Reality... Meaning if you get recalled, (Get in trouble while on Parole, and sent back to Jail) then you have to do whatever is left of your 8 years, instead of the 4 you had left before parole... I heard what they had said... I had learnt it's good to just listen to people and actually consider what they are saying, because Knowledge is Power, even if you don't use it...

But fuck that, nothing was stopping me from being/ getting out of here/ jail, first chance I got... I would take my chances with parole... If I could handle Jail, I could handle Parole... That's what I thought anyway... Well my plan worked, and here I was, Finally Free, and Feeling Good!!! I had walked into there/Jail, a young boy at the age of 21, with value and drinking issues... Well I won't say issues, but I was a product of my environment, and was taught wrong values... But you can't blame the older folk, they are just following the trend/ cycle...

Like I said before, I went in as a young boy, and now I'm on my first walk of Freedom, as a MAN... Prisoners, just as I did... As we do time/ are in the inside of jail, we make big plans for the Future... What we want to do in Life, and all we want to Achieve... At 21 I went in slim, and I was coming out all Muscular... You really had nothing else to do but workout inside jail, even though most guys are lazy... I was also into Football/ Soccer, and I knew if I applied myself I could get on the National Football team of Bermuda... And of-course I wanted to make money and Live lavish... But did I really have a Plan?? As I walk out of this Jail... NO... And that wasn't a bad thing, because I didn't think I could survive Jail and I DID... So, my next Obstacle was to Defeat Parole... My Plan/ Goal, was to be COMPLETELY FREE...

I look at My Obstacles, like I'm Running a Marathon... You can't actually say, what Exactly you going to do after the race, because you have to finish the race first... But do have some water waiting for you, when you do finish your Marathon... I don't even know why I put that in, I guess it means, you also plan ahead for when you do actually finish, even though finishing looks unlikely... But my battles seemed so Hard, just making it to the End of them would make me Happy... They/ The Babylonian System, won the First round, and Locked me up!!! (Bastards!!!)

And I just WON Round 2... My most Gruesome battle with Jail/ System... And now it was Round 3, Final round!!! Winning would mean Ultimate Freedom/ Glory... And losing would take me back to square one, which was back behind the walls and bars/ which feels like Death to me!!! Whatever is in store, I'll face it, Head on!!! It was a Blessing, I made it this far....

I walk down to the entrance of the Jail... It's a bus stop at the gate... I told my sister, I'll wait there at the bus stop for her to arrive... I know she is on her way, because I had just called her from my cell phone in my jail cell to confirm she was coming before I gave my phone away to one of my boys... I was leaving Jail, I didn't need it no more...

4

Even though I didn't tell the rest of the inmates/ prisoners, that I was cool with, that I was going home... Because even the ones close to you, will steal your stuff, and hide it... Then when you gone, they pull it out and act like it belonged to them all along... During my time inside, I went in many cells and saw pictures... I would know the person and ask the person about the picture and the guys later confess they don't know the people in the pictures and they took it out someone's cell when they were leaving... When at first, they had said it was their girlfriend or X... I'm also seen guys tell everyone that they are leaving to go home tomorrow or real soon, then they go to get breakfast, lunch, or dinner in the dining area or food hall, and when they get back to their cell, most of their shit Gone/ stolen... They were angry as hell, but who can they blame?? No one has seen anything...

The other Prisoners, wasn't going to get me like that... I told everyone, the Parole Board is sending me to T.L.C. the Transitional Living Center... This was just a building over the wall, but still within the jail compound... But you weren't looked at as Free from other prisoners, because guys get sent back in jail, from over there all the time... At the T.L.C. Building, you would be able to go out to work days, but you were back on their rules at night... So, since I told the prisoners I was going T.L.C. Building, they were not trying to steal my shit... I just told my real close boys, the ones I was giving all my shit to anyway... I guess it was their reward for keeping their mouth shut... Even when walking to intake to change into my regular clothes and leave jail... If someone asked where I was going, I'll answer T.L.C...

I mean Everyone was cool with me and all, but Fuck them... They weren't really my friends, they were cool, because they

"Had" to be cool…I'm not saying I'm the Baddest/ toughest guy, but I am not allowing myself, to be Disrespected or Abused in Any Way… Verbally or Physically, from talking shit, to hurting me in any way… I guess you can just tell when someone is soft, and you can tell when not to bother someone… And I have a Beast inside me, but I'm cool, so I wasn't worried…

See my Enemy while I was in Jail, from the beginning, to the End of this… Including Parole… Was never a next inmate, or person…I won't allow that… The enemy was the "SYSTEM…" The people that got us/ME, locked in here by their Babylonian system/ rules… I understand if you do something crazy, but the system was clearly taking advantage of people… For instance, My case, or anyone case… If I, or they, had the money at the time to bring in a Q.C. that's a Queens Council Lawyer… You had to pay heavy, because they from abroad… But if they had a Case in Court, and a Bermuda lawyer had the same case and same evidence… Having a Q.C. was the factor, that determines if you going to jail or not… It's just like they are respected more in the Bermuda courts… But like I said, "From the Beginning, the War was ON for Me!!!" So, "Any Chance," I got to break their rules and get over them, I definitely went for it… It was, "ME vs Them!!!"

Now the T.L.C. Building was not for me… When I sat in front of the Parole board, and they were trying to say, they think, I'll be better there, at the T.L.C. building… I'm saying to myself, "You Think Huh??… NO, that's Definitely not the Plan!!!" But I couldn't say that… They had my Freedom in their hands… So, I pleaded professionally, and I talked about all I'm done and accomplished in jail, and how that place, (the…TLC Building) won't be good for me…

I talked about how my family was waiting with a place for me and I'm got a good job waiting… I laid it all on the line, this was my last stand… All the while, I had my sisters address as my place to stay, but I wasn't going to stay there… I'll be staying at my mom's house in the Hood… I couldn't give a hood area address… They wouldn't have wanted to let me go free from Jail, knowing I'm going to live back in the hood… My job was also a Hoax/ Fake… My boy does own an air conditioning business, so I got him write/ type up letters saying, I'll be working with him, and how much I'll be making and that I'll be working at least 40 hours a week…

All the while, I wasn't leaving Jail to WORK… I was leaving jail to be FREE and Relax… It had felt like I was in War for the last 5 years… I needed a Vacation!!! All that Stress and shit I had to go through in Jail/ Prison, and now these people think I'm going out into the free world and slave again… Nah not me, I had other plans… VACATION….

Luckily the Parole board brought/ believed it all… It was a lot of other rules I had also… One was report to my Parole officer and follow all his rules like random drug (piss) test and whatever he decides as far as groups or whatever… I didn't have no curfew, that was good… I was also required to stay/ live at the address I provided, and let my parole officer know of any changes, because the parole officer also does home visits… I was also required to work a 40 hour a week job, like I mentioned… And don't be associated with any drugs or illegal substances… Most of all, stay out of All Trouble!!!

Failure to Comply with/ follow, all their Rules could result in the parole board Revoking my parole, and straight back Jail I would go… I understood, stay out of trouble Period… That was all I had to worry about… I could handle the parole officer, I had been dealing with the whole authority of the jail in control of me… Surely, I could handle one…

So, I'm standing at the bus stop just waiting for my sister thinking, taking in the Free world, and Feeling Happy… It's a nice sunny day… I'm just looking at the sights, and watching cars go by when they did… All the while I'm thinking to myself, "TUB, You Finally FREE!!!" I even said Out Loud, because it was no one around… "IM FREE! IM FREE! FINALLY!!!"

My sister finally arrives… She has my girlfriend/ special friend at the time, with her in the car… When the car stops, they get out give me a hug, and then we all get back in and head town… It felt good to sit back, with my arm around my chick, (that I had not fucked/ had sex with yet…) (smile), And my sister at the wheel of the car… I'm just enjoying the ride…

Me and My sister's plan, was to take me to my mother, and surprise her that I'm Actually Free from jail… My sister calls my mom, and asks where she is/ what's her location… She says she at the Bar, called Boat Club on Northshore… My sister tells her to wait there, she is coming there to see her… She has No Clue, that I'm free and we about to surprise her….

When we get there, we park and start to walk towards to the building/ bar… I walk in the side door, so it will be more of a surprise because from the side entrance she can't see me/ walk in the place/ walk up on her… My sister goes in the front entrance of the bar with my friend… When I walk into the bar, I say hello to my mom…. She spins around to look, because she recognises the voice… When my mom turns and sees me, she instantly cries and hugs me and is, So Happy… I say, "Mom I'm Finally Free!!! They gave me Parole and Let Me Go!!!"

She instantly orders a shot and we have a drink on my Freedom… (smile) From there My mom made a call and booked at Hotel, so me and my chick, could spend the night there and be alone… It was a Good first night out…

The next day, I went to meet my Parole officer… He was a tall, stocky guy… I knew his face, he used to be a police officer on the narcotics team… He said I was supposed to report to him yesterday, as soon as I got out/ was released from jail… I told him I didn't know that the rule was, "That as soon as a Parolee is Released from prison/ jail, he must report to his parole officer the same day…" He didn't make it a big deal though, he was a cool guy overall… He said, as long as I followed the rules, we won't have no Problems…

He reiterated (explained again) most of what I already knew… That I would be getting Pissed/ drug test every week, and they must be clean… He will do a home visit once a month, visit my job site, and he told me what day and time to report to him every week… I would see him for one hour a week, so he could check up on me and test me, plus make sure I'm staying on track… The drug testing was cool for me, because I wasn't smoking no weed, or any type of drug period… I only fucked with weed anyway… And for the home visit, that was cool, I'll just meet him there (at my sisters) and act like I stay there… And as far as job site, I was an apprentice at an Air Conditioning Business, and we are mobile, so when he ready to meet, I'll sort it out…

But I had No Plans in even working with my mate/ friend at his business… He already had my cousin working with him, and I just wasn't into that type of work anyway… I wasn't feeling, Any Work to be exact!!! I was Free Finally, So, technically, I Felt… "I WAS ON VACATION…"

Our meeting went smooth… Now I'm back in the car with my girlfriend, and my mom is driving us in my sister's car… Now before I got into my trouble/ went jail, I worked for the Health Dept. Pest Control… That's basically the Government owned pest control… I had worked there for about 4 and a half years… I started the job straight from high school, and I kept the job until I went jail… That could have been a promising career/ job, if I wasn't so into drinking and partying… I say that because, Since the Pest Control fell under the Health Department, we worked hands on/ side by side with the Health Inspectors… One of the inspectors was actually the Boss/ Manager of our department… His name was David, and he was always an honourable/ Fair man… And since they (the company/ dept) took a liking to me, and I was the young one straight out of school, they were somewhat grooming me for the future…

So instead of doing Pest Control work all the time, I would be sent out with different Inspectors on different days to learn things/ the stuff/ work they do… We would go to different restaurants and businesses and inspect their kitchens and areas... And if they weren't up to par/ the clean standard, they would have to close until the issues were sorted... Was many restaurants I helped inspect... And I also got to go to different hotels to inspect, and take water samples from their pools, to see if the level of chlorine was right, and also test the tap water of the kitchens... Restaurants had to have certain things stored, in the right place with the right temperature... Everything gets tested basically, and they all had many rules to follow...

They also started sending me to do the water samples and inspections alone, so their trust in me was growing... The people at the places, knew I was with the Inspector's team, so they would kiss your ass for a good report... Because this was the real deal... If the inspector felt your kitchen was too dirty... He closes that shit immediately, or it must be done or cleaned Now... I'm seen it happen... The inspector I was with for the day was not impressed with the business and made them close, until it was sorted...

I would also get to go with the Elite team in the Pest Control section, that went and inspected the Cruise Ships and Cargo/ Container Ships for any sign of rat droppings... If any droppings were found, you report it, and the ship/ vessel won't be allowed to leave Port/ the island because it hazardous or some shit... So, they must sort out the problem before we sign the papers of Pass, so the ship could leave...

One time I remember, I was doing one of these inspections on a cargo ship alone... I guess it was last minute, and the ship was scheduled to leave the island the next day... On my inspection of the areas of the ship, all were clear except for one... I saw mice or rat droppings in the Pantry/ store room... I just showed the captain and told him sort it out... And I told him consider himself Lucky, because by Law I could stop him/ the ship from leaving the next day... He was very thankful for the break... So, I signed the pass inspection sheet and gave it to the captain...

I wasn't trying to bother them people on the ship though... In my young immature mind, I was just passing time, waiting to knock off, so I can go link with my cousins, DEA, Ed, Shorty, and Ian, so we could drink some Rum and bullshit and smoke some weed... But yes, the job was ideal, if my mind was right at that time... So, since I worked for them years, they take out for pension or whatever, and then when I got in trouble, they were paying me half my pay to the outcome of my trial... Unfortunately, I blew trial... But anyway, after trial, they sent me a pay stub of my final pay... It was the amount of about 8 thousand 500 dollars... So, the whole time I was in jail, I'm thinking, well at least I'll have a start when I get out of jail...

My plan was, I wanted a Convertible... I had cut a picture of one, out of a magazine... And had it stuck it up on my cell wall, with the rest of my pictures people had sent me, the whole time I was in jail... So, as my mom is driving me in my sister's car, I say to her, "I want you/ her to take me to the Bank in St. Georges, so I can check out my bank account..." As soon as I said that, I sensed her mood change... She says, "TUB, don't get mad, but I forgot to tell you..." I'm like, "Ok, what is it??" She says, "Don't get Mad, but I had to use your Money..." I was confused, so I replied, "What you say??" She said, "Don't get Mad, but I used your

12

money to take your Aunty Myrna, away for her Cancer Operation…" I said, "What!!!" Then I said, "Don't say Nothing else… Let me think…."

I didn't want her to say no more, because she was right, I was about to get irritated/ mad… I wasn't violent or nothing, but she knew, I didn't/ don't deal with no bullshit… And if I was unhappy, my attitude alone was enough to drive anyone mad… I would just block you out if you irritated me, it was like you was dead to me… And she had felt my attitude wrath many times… I remember during my stint(time) in jail, me and her had an issue… I had requested something and instead of her just saying she couldn't do it… She would say it was being done, then when the time came it wasn't… So, me irritated now, I said to her at a visit in jail, I said, "Mother, you know I Love You… If you couldn't do it?? Why the fuck you didn't just say so?? I could have got someone else do it…"

I guess she didn't want to let me down… I was mad though, I said, "I think you need a break from seeing me…" I swear, I didn't let my mom see me for about 6 months, maybe less… After that punishment, if she couldn't do something, she let me know up front/ one time…

I wasn't the Typical Prisoner, I mean yes, I'm just stuck in jail like everyone else… But most people look at prisoners like they down, and you can treat them anyway you want, and the prisoner supposed to appreciate Half Ass Shit… Not me, I didn't give a Fuck!!! If you weren't keeping me happy, you had no need to see or hear from me… I wasn't soft, and I guess a break/ time away with no contact, makes people appreciate you… I'm had to cut off a few of my boys for a few months while I was inside also… With me you got to be a person of your word, or you out my world… After the breaks my boys acted right… Motherfuckers are going to show me I'm Appreciated Period… I didn't care if I was in jail or not…

So, I understood when my mom, kept saying don't get mad TUB, because I can be Irrational (unbelievable) sometimes, especially for her doing some stupid shit, like spend All my money… Now in my mind at the time, I'm thinking, "She just said she spent All Your Money… WTF… (What The FUCK) That's bullshit!!! But I am FREE, and "ALL" I wanted for the last 5 years is to be FREE… So, Fuck the Money really, I'm got Freedom… I could make more money…" So, I say to her (my mom), "Don't worry about it (the money), just still take me to the bank… I want to check the Account…"

We get to the bank… I wait in line to its my turn to be served… When I get to the counter, it's a guy serving me… I give him my id and the last pay stub I had got, which says 8 plus grand on it, and I say, "I want to check this account…" The guy takes the stub and starts to type on his computer… The man then says, "Sorry Sir, but this Account has been closed…" He said it in a way, that I knew this account has been closed for a long time now… I just shook my head in disbelief, and said, "Thanks…" And walked out the bank and back to the car…

When I got back in the car, I told her what the guy teller said quickly… My Mom was like, "Don't worry, you took care of me while you were in jail, so I'll take care of you now…" I guess she was talking about the Money… I said, "Don't worry about it… I'm Free…" I was happy With-In Myself, that I didn't let it irate me, but I thought to myself, my mom is Hardcore… I remember signing a paper for her while I was in jail, because she said she was selling the bike I owned when I went jail… And I also signed a paper, that gave her access to my trade union account because they took money out my account every week when I was working… But I don't know how she accessed the Bank, but so it Go… Got to Love Her… Without her there is No Me… She was definitely making sure, I start from scratch/ nothing though… Sold the bike, and closed the accounts… But I wasn't worried, FREEDOM was Finally here…

GERNEL L. DARRELL

...CHAPTER 2...
...VACATION/ DECISIONS...

$\mathcal{F}$REEDOM is Beautiful... I'm staying in a little apartment out court street with my mom... My girlfriend still around, but she was starting to get Over Protective, because of all the Attention I'm getting... People hadn't seen me for a while... Plus, when I went away, (to jail) I weighted about 170lbs and was slim... Now I was a built/ muscular 195lbs... Everyone would just stare at me, even little kids... I felt I wasn't that big, but I looked good and fresh... The everyday life was taking its toll on people, and I was in prison, preserving and training, so I was like a new face on the Block... Even the young new gangsters, had heard my Reputation and showed me Respect...

I was in VACATION Mode... My mother had a little rental cycle, so I would just use that/ ride that bike as transportation until I got my own transportation... My girl had a bike and was working also... She knew how I was though, and she knew I was all about making money, whatever way possible, I'm a Born Hustler... She also knew I was on my PIMP Shit... So, we had made an agreement that I could do my thing, as far as get money or whatever, but I couldn't touch any of the girls... That was cool for me, because whoever I had online/ in contact with, I had never touched anyway, and I had just got out of jail...

In the past, I have Never in my Life been faithful to one chick... I had met this special girl, while I was still on the inside of jail... I had called my cousin one day and he had an ace girl/ casual friend with him... I must have asked to speak to her, and we got on the phone and started talking... From that moment/ our first conversation I had her, and we were cool... She devoted herself to me and held it down for me while I was still on the inside... Even got my name tattooed on her... I thought the whole ordeal was promising... And since she respected My Pimping, maybe this could really work, I thought... So, I agreed to not touch No one else/ no other girls, and I was Serious...

I would get around girls and be So Tempted to Fuck them... And they would be Literally Begging for me to fuck them, or they would ask, can they at least suck my dick... This happened on a few occasions, but I would Refuse and not let No One touch me... In my mind, I'll tell myself, "No, you got a girl..." So, I would just fight the urge...

My girl never even knew I was seeing/ visiting other girls and getting money, I would make my moves when she was at work... But I guess she was just insecure... She just started accusing me of fucking girls... Then she would turn violent, and start attacking me... Coming at me screaming and swinging, trying to hit me and all... I would just grab her arms or whatever and get her calm down... But this shit just kept going on... One day when everything was calm, I'm telling the girl, "I have Not touched No One!!! And if she keeps Attacking Me, throwing shit at me... Hitting and trying to hit me, I'm going to get Fed Up one day, and she going to get it back!!!" I was WARNING her to Stop Fucking with me before I Lose Control and Get Nasty...

It got to a point where when she would start, she would hit me once, and then twice, and then one day I just punched her in the gut/ stomach... That calmed her ass down... But I should have known it would only get worst... I guess each time she felt she could take a little more... So, I knew once she started it was no good... Not saying I couldn't just beat her, but she was supposed to be my Baby, and in a Relationship, I didn't want to hurt her... I feel when it gets physical in a relationship, it's no good for no one... Plus I'm on Parole...I'm thinking, I'm leaving Drama behind me, this chick is just crazy...

After a few instances of that shit, I would just try Extra Hard to keep her happy, so we could avoid any drama... One night since my mom and me lived on court street... Me, my mom and my girl were in Swinging Doors Bar... Some girl must have been looking/ staring at me, I didn't see the girl looking, but my girlfriend did... So, here she goes... Trying to argue with me in the bar... And I already know, she is going to attack me, and I can't just smack her back in the bar, because I will look like the aggressor... (look bad Period) We had not really fussed in public before, but each second as she is trying to argue with me, I can feel her ready to hit me... She is getting loud and people are watching her little show... So, I'm thinking, I'm about to head out this bar...

I remember growing up from young on this same street... (Court street) I would always say it's always some type of entertainment on the street, from a couple fighting, to police chasing someone in car or bike... And here I am years later, and I'm the Fucking Entertainment, because of this crazy girl... SMH... (Shake My Head/ Unbelievable)

My mom was still at the bar also, so I told her I'm gone and headed towards the exit… My girl behind me the whole time, still trying to argue and talk about I was looking at girls or some shit… I'm thinking, I'm just going to get away from her, but also get away from her before she starts swinging on me, in front of the people watching…

I walk out the bar and up the street, and turn the corner out of every one's eye sight, she is following me the whole time, talking shit still… Once I hit the corner I just kept walking, I just wanted to be left alone… All I kept saying was, "I don't want to fuss!!!" and she still talking about me fucking someone… When I get up the street a bit, I guess she sees I'm not game for fighting tonight in the streets, so she attacks… Comes in screaming and swinging, anybody would think I had hit her already tonight how she is going on… I grab her to stop her from hitting me, and tell her calm the fuck down a few times… And then I push her away, and turn and continue to walk away from her… I cross the street, she still following me…

Next, I see a Police Wagon/ Jeep, come around the corner and drive cross us… The officers inside just look at me and continue to drive across slowly… I think to myself, if they would have come past 5 seconds ago, when she attacked, they would have taken Me for sure… This was not good!!! I had to get out of this shit!!! I'm on Parole also… I turned around and said, "You see the fucking Police!!! You trying to get me Locked up??!!!" I guess seeing the police truck and my words woke her up… She calmed down, and we walked back to my mom's place…

My mom was still out somewhere like regular, probably still at the bar… I started thinking about my night at the bar and seeing the Police a few seconds after she tried to attack me, and this girl, and all the Drama… I was having a drink, thinking about it all, I had also had a few earlier at the bar… I call the girl over to me, and stand up… I think to myself, "I'm going to teach her a lesson!!!"

I said to her/ my girl, "You want to Fight??" she didn't answer… I continued, "You always Attacking me like you're a Man, and like you Think, you can Beat Me or some shit!!!" Before she can answer, I punch her in her fucking stomach/ gut and she curls over in pain… I say, "You always fucking with me, like I'm some pussy…" And I slap her across her face hard… She stands up to hold her face in disbelief that I slapped her… I then give her another gut shot/ punch her in her fucking stomach again, she also curled over again… I said, "Don't Ever Fuck with Me!!! I am Not, the One to Play With!!!" And I went back to doing whatever I was doing…

After that night, since I Lost Control… In the next few days, I told the girl, "We can't be in a Relationship no more…" I said, "We can still be cool as friends, but we got to take a break… As far as the Relationship, it had been about 6 or 7 months of nothing but drama and now it physical, I'm on Parole, I don't need this…" She didn't like the idea, but the decision was Final…

I then left her at the apartment to sort her things she had there, so she could go, because she was basically living there with me… This crazy bitch packs her belongings, and then turns on all the water taps in the apartment, including the tub and leaves… She tried to flood the place out… My mom came home just in time, as the water was spilling all over the floor… When I got back home she told me how she found the place flooding…

Well my girl, was gone and we were done so I just left it as that… She(my girl) would still call me, and she knew I needed my hair braided, so she offered to do it… Plus around this time I was going down my boy Ken's house a bit more, since the girl wasn't around, and somehow I thought it be a good idea, to start smoking weed again… (get to that part of the story later) My x-girl smoked weed also, so I felt it was a win, win situation… Get my hair done and some free smoke/weed… She began to use that angle, to always see me… So, before you knew it, I was borrowing this girls bike when she was at work again… It was a better and newer bike than my mom's rental… She just said she don't want no girls on her bike… Ok, that was fair enough, I just won't take no girls on her bike…

One day I drop my x-girlfriend to work, so I can have the bike for the day… I didn't really have nothing planned for the day… So, I was just chilling in my hood… My little sister calls me and asks if I'm got trans, she wants a lift somewhere… So, I go pick her up to take her… As I'm riding, I get a call from my X girl, she says, "I just got a call and you got a girl on my bike…" I said, "I picked up my little sister a second…" She knew my little sister and all… She replied, angrily, "I said No Girls on my bike…" She continues, "Bring me my bike…" I say, "Ok, I'll drop off my sister n come…" She said, "NO!!! Bring it Now!!! Else I'm calling the police and say you stole/ took it…" I said, "OK…" I thought to myself, this girl is a Psycho/ Crazy…" I wasn't that far from her job, I took her bike directly to her…

When I took her the bike, I told her, "If she ever in any Danger, she can call me, but other than that, We Are Done for Real!!!" And I gave her the Key to her bike and left... Police threats were a No- No, in My World... From there on she would call and ask to do my hair or bring me some smoke and I would refuse and tell her I won't be taking calls from her no more... From there on, she would just call "Over and Over" from a private number and not say nothing on the line... I would know it her because I would get fed up with the continuous calls and I would finally say, "You must love me!!! Your calling and not saying Fucks!!! You like my Damn voice??" I would say that into the quiet phone... And she would finally answer and say, "I don't want you..." I'm like, "So, it is you calling over n over and not saying nothing, like you Crazy!!!" There was no End to this, so I changed my phone number to lose all contact with them people... We just couldn't see eye to eye...

As all this is going on, and finally behind me, all my focus went into football (soccer)... I was playing with my childhood team, Boulevard Blazers... The white/ Portuguese guy ROBELLO, was the coach at the time... I was training hard, and the coach picks his 16 players for the weekly game...I was always in it, (the 16) but it was like he didn't want to play me in the games... This had been happening for a while, this coach putting me in his team but not giving me no time on the field... Then it was a cup game, the game went into over-time, and I was a substitute... Everyone on the field was tired, so I knew if I went on the field now, I'll be the star... I asked the coach to put me on the field, and he just said hold on... He never put me on, he just let the time run out, and said next time he'll put me in… I felt that was a foolish move as a coach, but so it Go…

After that game, the next time at training, I ride in on my mom's rental cycle… I look at the coach's car, it's a BMW black convertible… I say to myself, "TUB, you need to go make some money!!! Your Fucking, with this coach that don't want to play you, and you riding a rental bike… Go make some money, get nice things, then you can focus on football… I'm training 3 times a week and game Sunday… But I'm on bench whole time, that wasn't no fun… I'll be back…" And I turned the bike around and went back to the hood… I'm got to figure out how to make some Paper/Money…

Back to the Smoking, I mentioned earlier… Hanging around my boy's yard, and everyone was smoking… At first, I was strong and refused to smoke… As time went by, I heard of some stuff called Quick Flush, that you could drink it, and drink water and the Weed won't show up in the piss test the Parole officer would give me… In hopes that it will work, I went and brought some from the health store… So, I'll already have it when needed…And from there I was smoking… Back to smoking Weed again….

Now it was time for my visit to the parole officer, I was seeing him every 2 weeks now… I knew how to play the good boy role, so our meetings were cool… I looked at them visits as my one hour of jail… But this one would be different, because I was smoking weed now, which is against my parole rules… But I also got the Quick Flush, so I'll be cool… I drink the liquid, it was the size of a regular juice or soda bottle, and cost like $20 a bottle… I drank it about an hour before my visit/ test like the bottle said I should…

And then I tried to drink as much water as I could… They say that you're supposed to piss/ urinate a bit before you actually pee to give your sample…

I get in the meeting and all is going as usual, and now it's time to take the urine/ piss test… We walk into the bathroom, and he watches, me piss in the cup, he is standing behind me… I pass him the cup and wash my hands like regular… He puts the sample test we use in, and we wait for the readings… I'm Praying in my mind, please be clean… Even though I just smoked a joint of weed right before taking the liquid over an hour ago…

A few seconds later, he looks at me and says, "The test is saying, its traces of marijuana(weed) in your system…" I'm instantly in shock, I hoped I'll get lucky and the drink would work!!! My mind Races, to think of an excuse… I say, "I'm been around guys that were smoking, it has to be second hand smoke!!!" I convince him, it must be that… He sends the urine/ piss test to their lab, to confirm the reading of marijuana… I'm thinking, "What the Fuck, how did I go wrong??" It's probably because I was rushing the liquid to work… I'm got to drink it earlier next time, and drink more water…

So, I played like I was stunned about the whole weed showing up thing… After the parole visit, I went back to the health store and purchased more of the Quick flush for next time… Then I went back to my life of smoking and being free, and thinking of ways to make more money… The 2 weeks had passed, and it was parole visit time again… I didn't learn, I went through the same last minute/ hour before drinking the quick flush, and just try drink some

GERNEL L. DARRELL

water routine, that I done the last time before the visit...
When we got into the visit, he says let's go test you first...
He tested me again, and just like 2 weeks ago... Dirty for
weed again... I say it must be the second-hand smoke, and
shrug my shoulders like I have no clue... He doesn't say
much, just disposes of the test, and we head back to his
office...

When we get back in his office... He says, "The test is not
sensitive enough to pick up second hand smoke, so you can
stop saying it... You must be smoking!!!" He continued, "It
takes 6 weeks for weed to get out your system... So, I give
you 6 weeks and I'll test you again... And if your test is
Dirty, you are going to SEE THE PAROLE BOARD!!!"

Hearing them words, shook me up!!! I thought to myself,
"Yes, you like to smoke weed, but you don't want to wind
up back jail because of smoking weed..." So, my plan was,
to smoke for 3 more weeks and then stop, and use 3 weeks
to get it out my system...

I smoked for the next 4 weeks, and then said, "That's It!!!" It
wasn't worth the chance of jail... So, I had 2 weeks to get it
out my system... After the 6 weeks had passed and we met,
he didn't test me... I guess he was giving me 2 extra weeks
because I saw him every 2 weeks... So, when he finally
tested me again, I was done smoking and my piss test was all
clear... My Freedom was more Precious... It wasn't easy,
just making myself just stop like that, but the thought of
being back in jail, was enough to give me the strength...

I had been out over a year and a bit now, and I would still
have Nightmares of being Locked up... In my dreams, I
would be in the unit or another part of the jail, or in a cell

26

and I'll be pleading with the officer, saying, "How did I get back in here!!! This is against my Human Rights!!! I haven't done Nothing!!!" In another dream I would wake up and be in a cell on a bunk… I would instantly say to myself, this is a Dream, and try to lay back down and wish myself out of it, but no the dream here to stay… I would "think" I went back sleep and when I try to wake again… I get up in dis-belief, I'm in jail, so I think it Real…

When I finally wake up from the horrible dreams, and realize I'm actually Free… Tears come to my eyes… If I was lucky, I could make myself wake up, as soon as dreams start… I see I'm in jail, and instantly say, "Fuck this shit, Wake up now!!! And make myself wake up (Lol)… My mind would Fuck with me Big time, with dreams of being back in Jail…

Now it was time to put my effort towards making Money… I was still on Vacation, so I wasn't trying to make no one's time… So, I looked to the streets… Now my boys house where I chill out at, those guys are into computers, and they work, but they more mobile and have their own business, so someone is always home… But around this time, My Big OG, "LOGY" had just came out of jail… He was always in and out of jail for something… From beating someone in the streets, to fighting the cops… It was no end to him, he was HARD all the way… We had always been cool, as a little nigga coming up, I would see him out in the hood… He had some Sick/ Crazy Pitbull dogs, that would bite you, if you got close to them or him…

Back in the day, I would roll with his younger cousin, and me and his younger cousin would take the dogs out walking… Everyone feared the Dogs… You had to make sure you didn't walk close to people, because the dogs would just bite Anyone... They were Sick/ Real crazy dogs... I don't know how he got them so crazy... Some people thought he actually gave the dogs drugs, because they would attack cars and trucks and shit... But he later told me, he just trains the dogs well, and does it at night and alone, so the dogs just listen to him... I think he also kept crazy dogs for when the police come and try to buss his house... They knew they couldn't just barge in with them dogs in there...

We became much tighter, when he passed through the Pen(Jail) when I was up there... I remember when I got my first tattoo... I went and shouted to him across the fences because he had just got to jail and was on the other side over Remand... Remand is where they hold you while you are awaiting trial... They keep guys in remand separated from the population side of the jail... It was basically 4 sections to the jail... SEGREGATION, MAXIUM SECURITY, REMAND, and POPULATION... So, I shouted out to my Big HOMIE... The cell they had him in was facing the population side... I showed him the tat on my arm, and said I got my first tattoo... He shouts back, "What it says, "HARDKNOCKS??" I was like, no the Hood... M-TOWN and my name... HARDKNOCKS coming later...

In jail I was very crafty... One day I sent Logy some goodies from canteen, and I asked the Worst officer, could he drop the bag to him... The officer was a real Dick... Officer D... from one of the Caribbean islands... He was an Asshole, but I didn't mind him, he was by the book... I preferred to know where the officer coming from, rather an officer playing cool one day and fucked up the rest... Officer D., was straight fucked up, and I respected that... And he wasn't a bad guy, his personality was cool, but don't get caught doing anything wrong, and don't expect any breaks from him… No extra time out your cell, no extra time on recreation, nothing…

Now little did the officer know, I was using him to carry "Shit" to my boy, that the officer would Love to find… The officer checked the context of the bag, and I played cool like everything was regular… Once the bag was dropped to my boy, I called out to him and told him look in this or that… When he found what I was talking about, he was like, "Your crazy, getting Officer D… deliver the bag with a stash in it…" I just laughed and said, "Fuck him…" Me and Logy, had a lot more, run ins inside, because at that time, I had/ was cool with the girl that worked up in the prison offices… So, I was getting all different type stuff…

Now back to the streets… Logy just came out of jail, and I basically, immediately started hanging out with him… Word on the streets were, he had Beef with the 2 leaders of the young goons, that were running around in the streets… The young wild goons were young boys, that called themselves Park Side… I was hearing about all the crazy shit they were doing on the streets when I was up top in jail… But one of their so-called leaders was from Middle Town/ My Hood, so all the youths teamed up and became a strong force in the streets…

Now since I'm been out of jail, I had been out clubbing with the young goons, they were cool and Respected me… The night went smooth, with no violence… But everywhere we went, someone would say to me on the low, that I shouldn't be hanging around them guys, they are trouble… I guess everyone was afraid/ timid of when they were around because you never knew what would happen… Because at times they were known to do crazy/ reckless shit…

At one of the clubs that night, I was in the bathroom with the other so-called leader of the Park Side Gang/ crew… They called him Prince… We were about to walk out the bathroom and he says to me, "TUB, I'm heard about your Reputation and gave me my Respect…" So those guys (the goons) were always good with me… They hung right on the street, outside the building my mom lived in on court street also… If they were out on the street drinking Hennessy, (the type alcohol they liked to drink) they would want me join if I was out there, or if I was passing through… I'll drink a little, a shot or 2, and then dip out/ leave and go where I was going or whatever…

Now Logy is out of jail, and I'm hearing him and some of the goons are Arch Enemies… Especially Prince and Logy, don't like each other… The young niggas were cool, but my Loyalty is with my OG Logy… This nigga has made Legendary status, All Alone in the past, to become King of The Streets/ King of the Block/ King of Court Street… Yes, the young boys were making a name for themselves, but it was 30 plus of them… Logy was feared by the streets, Alone… Just a Boss… Around this time, hanging with him, is when I guess I officially, entered the Hard-Knocks Family… The way I saw it, it wasn't no Real Beef with the young boys like that… They had had an altercation before, when I was locked up, but since I'm bin out, it was just known they didn't like each other… They weren't trying to kill each other…

Now hanging/ being around Logy was like a "Next Level" of Hood living… It started slowly at first, I was just around chilling at his yard… So, I'm telling him how I want to make some money… I knew about the Hussle game, start at $50 buy a turner rock… Which you could sell and get $80 to $100 back in return… If u got $80 back, you buy another turner, and next time get 2 and so on… Or if you made $100, buy 2 one time and keep going to you got $350 to buy an 8 ball… An 8th of an ounce, and just keep hustling to you got money to buy bigger or enough money to buy what u want… It was a lot of work, in it though… You had to deal with the drug smokers, that wanted a lot for a little bit of money… They were trying to hustle you… Then u had the Police to worry about… Playing the hustle game could get you in jail quick… The Police are very much on top of every area, and they know what's going on most times, plus they pay informers for info, so at any moment they could come for you… So, u had to be super carful… It is actually scary, the unknown of hustling… You also have people trying to rob you, and its long hours, and sometimes its dead quiet… But all in all, it was try it out, or get a job… And I was still on Vacation, so I didn't want to be making no one's time yet…

I knew the Theory and had hustled a little bit before jail… I guess hustling is just natural growing up in the hood… Now at this time, little did I know that my OG had links and connects and would do his hustling thing sometimes… So, my OG says, I could get a ball and sell it and give him back $300… I agreed, and my hustling began… He was also giving the same deal to his cousin, so I had company on the hustling spot… We would just chill right in the yard of the house, and people that wanted crack would just come there... I went on a schedule, I would hustle in the yard all night, and when morning comes, I'll go down to the corner, down the hill, where my next boys from the hood, hustled days... I'll go down to their spot and grab any morning sales coming cross... As soon as I saw the first police car or van, I would then move my spot up Top road of Middletown, by my aunties house... And at night, I let the people know where I'll be in the day time... And when I got tired, I'll go down to my boys Ken and Ty's house and go lay down and sleep...

I stayed on my grind/ hustle and eventually Money and Gold came... I would tell people that wanted to buy drugs, "The only thing I want is money or gold, no TV's and bullshit..." Gold was a chance that it wasn't real, so I'll try my best to test it good before I accepted it... Most times it was real... A few times I got some fake shit, so I kept a clear bottle of bleach close... Drop that shit in bleach, after a little while you could tell if it was real... Plus people knew my Big OG, didn't play... So, they respected his house and area... I was respected also, of course, but I was new to steady hustling... But like with anything, money comes and goes... And it always seems like deals come to the hood when money is low... I was making money but spending and paying for re-up... So, I decided to save up, so when I re-up, I could buy my own, and all the money I make be Mine... And that's what I did...

Now the money I was making was mine... I had rings on all fingers, and this was when the deal of my first bike came... It was a purple V80, and it was sprayed all pretty and nice... I had to have it... The guy only wanted $500 for it but my money was low... I think I had just brought more drugs to turn... I called my boy Fab, from east and borrowed $400, and I brought the bike for $500... I paid him back soon after, and I had my first bike... Now all this time, when I had nothing, it was ok to go sleep down my boy's house, but I guess since he sees a little gold and now a bike, I sensed a little vibe from him... But I had no time to pay him any mind... He has basically made it, got his family backing him and all... I just had to stay focused... Made me think friends are weird sometimes, like to see you down...

I kept my routine up, I was going to make it... I refused to go out and party, I needed to get my money up... Things were working out though, so next I brought a red station wagon car, from my boy Biggie, for a price I couldn't refuse... And it seems like right after that, maybe even the next few days, I then brought another bike from my next brethren... The car needed a little work, so I ended up trading it for an Expensive sprayed up SCOOPY bike... So now I'm got 3 bikes, money coming in, and Me and Logy, rolling hard... I started to go out with him a bit more...

Rolling with him, felt like the High Rollers Life... Whenever we went to any bar, he would slap a Big Stack on the bar, and we would take shots of Chivas Regal all night... I needed chaser, so I would drink beer chaser, or Chivas and Ginger-ale soda as a drink for chaser... He would always pay for everything for all of us, whoever was there with us... Me, Logy and Mad Ed, would go west, and hit up all the bars and shit... Other regular days, we would chill in the hood, drinking bottles of Crystal, or Don P... Some days go half and half on a bottle, other days we would each buy our own bottles... Them bottles were $150 for each/ for 1...

I got into drinking all the expensive shit from chilling with him… He refused to drink anything but Chivas, Don P. or Crystal… I didn't care really, I would drink beer and cheap alcohol like vodka also… Logy had brought a little red car for his mom, he brought himself a New Kia Jeep… This was when they were new to the island, and it was also my first time driving one, when I drove his… He then brought a BMW station wagon, that shit was like an airplane inside… Another first for driving one… After a few months, I started to want my own car…

So, I went in an even deeper hustle mode and was looking online at cars at the same time… I saw this nice White Renault Convertible, I wanted it Bad!!! It would be mine, I promised myself… I hustled Hard… Everything was for sale, if the Price was right, you could get it… The shirt off my back, rings I had, bikes, I was willing to sell it all… I wanted that car… The car was 21 Thousand dollars… I hustled my ass off, but I finally reached my goal… The car was probably 10 years old, but was kept in a garage and looked brand new… I LOVED IT…

Soon after that Logy was going to buy a Peugeot hard top convertible for about 30 thousand, but he didn't buy it in the end, but I did get to drive the car when we took it for the day, to test it out… Life was cool, chilling in the hood, making a little money, and just rolling with my niggas… I think to myself, "I'm came along way since Jail… VACATION IS GOOD…"

...CHAPTER 3...

MAINO...K.O.B. IN BERMUDA

I'm bin free like 2 years now, nothing much is really going on, still chilling with my OG, making money and partying and shit... I'm still got up the charade of me working... I just got a new P.O. (parole officer) it's this guy Mr, M... He was from Canada, and married a Bermudian girl... So, since he was a foreigner, he was on the tip, that he got to show the system, that he started working for, that he was needed and could do a good job... So, he tried to be extra hard on the guys/ X- prisoners he had under his watch... I wasn't worried, he was Not going to stop my Show, or my Vacation, that I was still on...

During this time, I had hooked up with an old friend I had met just before I went jail... I always thought she was Absolutely Beautiful... Too make a long story short... She got pregnant and I was due to have a baby... This freaked me out, because I thought I'll never have children... Now the P.O. trying to tell me, I need to take a child parenting class... I Refuse... One I don't need it and 2, I know how to take care of kids and 3, that will take up more of my free time... I escaped the class he wanted me to do...On March 6th my precious baby girl was born... Now before this day, Life was only about Me, but now I had a little baby to protect from the Cold World...

To be honest, I didn't want no children, and if I had a baby I wanted a boy… But I think God knew my heart was Cold, so he decided to soften it a bit, and give me the Greatest Gift ever, my baby girl… Now my world was me and the little one, and I felt like fuck everyone else/ the rest of the world, per say… I mean I cared about people, but she is the only person, I have to consider and protect… My little princess… I thank God for her everyday…

On the other side of things, in my Hood Life… With my OG when we go out, it seems like I'm got to be a protector… Not protect Him, but Protect the World from him… At any second, he would attack people… If he didn't like you, or you owed him money, it was Trouble… It could be a small amount, he didn't care, if he was in the wrong mood, Any One could get it…

One time we went Smoking Joes tattoo place… This is when he had his shop out by Arnolds… As soon as we walk in the door, My OG is attacking a guy, smacking him up… We weren't even fully in the place yet… It was me, my OG, and his Big Bro, OG K… OG K. was a killer also… In the younger days, he must have killed their mom's boyfriend, for hitting their mom in America… I see my OG attack someone as soon as he opens the door, I'm walking behind him and as soon as I see this, I think to myself, I wonder who owes him money this time… When I see who it is, I'm not surprised at the attack… It's Prince, his Arch Enemy… Smoking Joe said to them, "Respect my Business, go outside if you guys want to fight!!!" They both come out the tattoo place and start fighting… My OG swings a punch and it lands cross the jaw, so Prince goes in for the grab, to pick up and slam his opponent… He grabs logy and tries to slam him on the ground, but it didn't exactly work how he planned... They scuffle and fight a bit more and OG K. goes in and breaks it up... Prince gets up and runs off...

I just watched, it was no need for my involvement... When we drove out, Prince was at the end of the lane looking in the mirror at his lip... Him and my OG, exchanged threating words again, and we were off... A few days later, I saw PRINCE(R.I.P.) at a bar... It was BOOTIE's spot he had on front street before... I was standing at the bar, and I noticed someone standing behind me... So, I look back to see who it is, and its Prince, I pay him no mind and look back forward... I guess he was looking for a Scared reaction... He was with all his niggas and shit... He stands next to me at the bar... I said, "Look, you 2 been Beefing before I even got out, that shit ain't/ has not, got nothing to do with me..." He replied, "Aight/ Ok cool, because, I saw that day, you didn't get into it, when you could have..." He brought me a drink/ shot, and we left it as that...

Ya, I wasn't playing no Fighting Game, with them guys... I told my OG, if we go War, then we going to war For Real... No going beat them up bull shit, and the next day, I'm got to fight like 30 guys... He had access to them things, (tools) me and OG K. told him, we were down for whatever he chose... It never went no further than that though...

Logy was also into music... So, he started a promoting company, HARDKNOCKS Music Promotions... He then decided to bring the New Artist PAPOOSE to Bermuda... He had it all lined up... The Promo was playing on radio and all, and before the show could happen, he gets locked back up and had to cancel the show...

When he got back out of jail, he decided to bring the Artist MAINO from Brooklyn into Bermuda for a show... The Hi Hater song by MAINO had just came out, and was Hot... The show went down as planned somewhat... It was cool to be hanging around a Rap Star, that I had watched on music videos... And also knowing the dude MAINO just done 10years in jail, and came out and became a Big Rapper... That showed me that they, (the system) can lock us up, but in the end the Choice is ours what we want...

I don't get all, Star-struck, so it was all routine for me, just chilling with my nigga Logy... Logy had MAINO staying at the Hamilton Princess Hotel on Front street... I was all up in the hotel rooms, and all around the pool with MAINO and his crew... They all seemed like regular niggas to me, because My Life was Rich... Not in the monetary sense completely, but I was making a little money on the streets, and being able to live good and buy whatever I want... But you can never have enough money... Parole was cool, I still looked at the meetings as my 1 hour of jail, every 2 weeks now... I had my Car, White Soft-Top Convertible... A car I always dreamed of, and GOD had Blessed me with a Precious Baby Girl and My FREEDOM!!! My Life was Definitely Rich...

I was around the Star Rapper and his crew a lot, but the high light for me was one day after being out by the pool, we ran into some girls in the hotel... They see MAINO and recognise him and they go crazy... We invite the girls back to the hotel room... So, we all chilling in the hotel room, it had to be like 8 to 10 chicks... And most are on MAINO trying to talk to him and ask him questions and shit... Bermudian girls love American guys... So, one of the chicks say, "I don't want MAINO, I want him, and she pointed at me... We were all drinking and shit, so we just laughed at her comment...

Logy always had, Don P., Crystal or Chivas, and since the rappers were here, he done it up Bigger... You know me, I'm just chilling, and rolling with my dog/ nigga... I don't know what I said to the chick, that said she wanted me and not MAINO, but a little later, I'm got this girl in the bathroom of the hotel room, and I'm thinking, I'm going to fuck this girl... If you want me keep it real, like I do... I remember our conversation a little... I was ready to fuck her, sucking on her tits, and my dick was hard... She started talking about if I want to fuck her, I must eat her pussy first... I said, I really don't do all that, so I'll pass... But I knew she was too horny, and she wanted me... My fingers were all in her pussy already... I just put on a condom, and put her up on the sink of the bathroom in the Hotel room, and fucked her good... I thought to myself, I just met this sexy girl and fucking her already, Thank God for MAINO... Lol... Not saying that don't always happen for me, because it did on a regular, but that what crossed my mind, when I had her in the bathroom...

Me and the girl, ended up becoming close after that night... She later told me, that first night, she thought I was an American and with them guys from away, that's why she let me hit it, the first night... But I knew better, girls use any excuse to not look like a slut... But for me, I know most chicks, don't just give up the pussy/ give themselves away one time/ on the first night... They usually make the guy wait for sex... So, if the mood and timing right, and they break their Rules and give themselves to me... It makes me

Feel Special, and in return I treat them with respect still... And it usually goes far in relationship... 90% of my long-term relationships, I had sex with them, first night or first chance we got... And it has the opposite effect, if the girl wants to hold out like her pussy gold... The longer you make me wait, the less I want it... Now I know, why most guys just play the roll until they get the pussy and then they gone... Me I don't have time for all that, if I'm not getting it, I'm gone...

The next day MAINO had an interview with Ms. Thang, at hot 107 radio station, which he wore a hotel robe to the interview, because he just came from swimming in the hotel pool again this day... Ms. Thang was looking cute and classy as always, just how she did back in her B.I. (Bermuda Institute) School days... Her and MAINO, connected/ vibed one time... As they chopped it up/ talked on the radio, I was just sitting in the room chilling and listening... I thought to myself, how I have always thought, if Ms Thang, was to write a book, all she would have to do is send One copy to Opera, and she would be a Super Star... She a Star now, but I think the book be interesting, and make her a Super Star... Especially if Opera gets involved...

That night we guys all decided to go to a club down front street, so MAINO can see the Bermuda Clubs and vibe... I was on a High, met that shorty last night, now we in the club and all the girls can't believe MAINO is Actually in Bermuda... And I'm rolling with him, so you know they are looking at me like a Big timer... I'm been drinking all day, and feeling good...

Inside the club, we get drinks from the bar and the guys decide to post up at the back of the club... Me, I'm on the

Hunt… As we all talked about last night, before we came to the club tonight… MAINO said to me, "Them girls were cool last night, but a little too happy/ immature for him…" I felt him, because they were a little too excited he was there, and acting all giddy and shit… So, I don't think he fucked any of them… I was thinking, I'm going to get him some pussy tonight, or at least make sure, he meets lots of girls tonight!!! I had asked him, if he had Fucked a particular girl, I had seen in his Hi Hater music video… I thought she was kind of fine/ sexy… And he confirmed to me that he had fucked the one I thought was fine… He had good taste like me, I thought…

So, now we in the club and girls are speaking to him and shit, but Bermudian girls won't actually holla at a guy, like an American chick would… Like say she wants to get with you… They play all modest and you got to holla at them, if you really want to hook up… So, I'm on the dance floor, dancing with girls, or should I say getting all close to them wining them up and shit, and then I'll say to the girls, "Lets, go meet my friends…" Then I'll just take the girls to the back of the club, to LOGY and MAINO and his crew, and introduce the chick so she can get to know them, so they can see if anyone connects… Then I was gone again to find more… I don't know what it was, I usually Can talk to the girls at bars/ clubs and not get rejected, some say I'm sexy, others think I'm cute and all that bull shit… Others are taken and let me down nicely, and once in a blue I get flat out rejected just like any other man I guess…

But this night, not One girl refused my invite/ advances to dance, or if I wanted their number, or my invite to go back to them guys… I remember thinking to myself, "I Can't be

Stopped!!! It was like I'm got that MAINO Juice tonight…
Like, Pimp Juice that I have tatted on my back, but MAINO
Juice tonight, because I was partying in the Club with him…
I was on All the girls, and it was like I couldn't lose… At the
bar, dance floor, anywhere I saw a chick, I thought was fine
or sexy, I was On That, one time!!!

I had just taken a girl to meet MAINO, LOGY, and the guys
to talk, and I go back to the dance floor… And it is this sexy
white chick dancing… I go close, and dance with her a little,
and touch/ feel all over her ass a bit… She was definitely
feeling me!!! I had a gold chain and Jesus piece pendant on,
that I had brought in the hood, so I was shining like regular
and looking fresh… I back off from the chick a little and
take a step back, so I can look at her again, and I think to
myself, "Fuck/ Damn she nice/ very Sexy…

I go to the bar, get a drink, make a little round/ circle,
around the club… I go check them guys, LOGY, and
MAINO and his boys, see what they up to… They still just
chilling in the club listening to the music and talking to girls
and others are checking out the girls basically and dancing…
I go back dance floor, the sexy white chick still dancing… I
go close and dance to a rap song, just trying to get close to
her and feel her body some more really… The Song ends,
and I play it cool, and just step back, the whole time I'm
thinking, she would be nice for Me, but I'm thinking of My
Niggas…

Because I know if MAINO hits it, he be Happy, and it
would also make LOGY look good because he brought him
down to the island… I Couldn't let MAINO leave Bermuda
without getting some leg/ pussy on the island… Not saying
he hadn't hit something already, or couldn't pull it off on his

own, because I wasn't around him 24/7, but I wanted to make it happen/ play a part in something… Not saying he will get to hit this sexy one right here, but it's definitely worth a try…

She was Fine as Hell, and had all the guys in the club watching her… Guys around the dance floor were looking at me like a King, because I wasn't scared to approach her, and plus I was dancing with her and feeling her up… She was that fine!!!

Some next niggas/ guys, who were in the club by the dance floor… When I stopped dancing with her and stood back… It was 2 of them, they said to me, she ain't/ is not going to pay u no mind, we just gave her pills… I guess they meant x-ecstasy… I didn't know if they were serious or not, because it didn't look like they were with the girl, and I was all over her when dancing and she seemed like she was feeling me, not every other nigga on the dance floor… But usually a girl will stay with a guy that's got x-pills if she likes pills…

I wasn't worried… I thought to myself, "These guys don't know, it's No Way in hell, this fine ass girl going to get away from me!!! Especially not tonight, "I'm on Fire," with that MAINO/ PIMP JUICE…" Plus I was feeling nice, so I was ON… So, I replied to the guys standing there, I said, "You think so?? You'll see…"

I could already feel that the girl was feeling my vibe… Next song started, and I went and started wining on her sexy ass again and said, "Let's Go meet my boy, MAINO the Rapper from America…" She put out her hand, I grabbed her hand gently, and off I was hand in hand, walking this Fine Bitch/ Lady, to my Niggas… About time we got to the guys, she was basically hugging my arm… I know they saw me coming, I was shining and with this trophy on my arm, shit was on… I took her over to LOGY and MAINO and introduced them, she sat down next to MAINO, and they instantly start talking, I know he thought she was Sexy… She had to be the Sexiest Girl in the club that night, and then I was off again looking for more interesting people… The vibe was right, music good, alcohol flowing, money in my pocket, and I was all over the club dancing with girls and having a Blast!!!

I don't know what was said, but MAINO's Game must have been Tight because all I remember, at the end of the night we were all back in the hotel room, (we guys and some girls) and talking about how MAINO, is fucking the white girl in the next hotel room… Logy had to go in the next room to get a bottle of Don P., so I made sure I went to… I had to see this, for myself… (Lol)

We walk in the next hotel room to grab the bottles quickly, and MAINO got the girl on the bed fucking her from behind… He had on his boxers, but she was completely naked, Tits/ Breast all out… Damn at that moment I wish I was fucking her instead of grabbing this damn alcohol lol… He just looked over to us and smiled, we grabbed the bottles turned and went back out the room… I think MAINO's right hand man, went in the room next…

It was a Good Night, I thought to myself, at least you can say, "You got MAINO some Pussy…" Then I headed out… I don't know if I went home or check an ace girl, but I had to go get some pussy myself, the thought of him fucking that sexy white chick was too much, I had to go hit something myself…

44

Other than that, nothing really stood out to me, except when Logy had the actual show up Dockyard, at Snorkel Beach Park... When I think back, I swear my nigga JIMBO from West was there at the show, I was standing by him while MAINO went on stage... The show was tight, MAINO done his thing on stage... All I remember was the moment at the end of the night, MAINO was telling me bring a next white girl to the hotel... I had met her that night and had her in my car, with the top down... She was off the cruise ship in dockyard and I was to meet MAINO and LOGY and them guys at the hotel in town... MAINO saw that thing in my convertible car outside the club in the street and said bring her Hotel... I know what he meant, he wanted to hit it... And I was going to deliver again...

My Game was tight like that, but I never made it Hotel... I was Too Drunk... I shouldn't have even been driving... Once I started driving this white girl to the hotel, I realize the hotel is too far and I'm too drunk... So, I just pulled over somewhere quiet and tried to fuck the white girl myself... I ended up giving up on trying and just dropped her back off to the cruise ship... MAINO headed back America and Blew Up!!! He became even a Bigger Star Now, and his New Title is, K.O.B. (King of BROOKLYN...) Got his own dance called the Millie Rock... I must mention, UNCLE MURDA since I mention Brooklyn, if u a Gangster u must listen to his shit... UNCLE MURDA and MAINO doing it big... PAPOOSE is hot also... They all from Brooklyn New York...

After that things pretty much went back to normal... Chilling in the hood and hustling... Now I'm looking like a Hood Legend... I survived Jail and I'm looking like I'm on

Top of the World... One of my hood niggas, BRIGGIE from Middle town, we had grown up together and he was like my brother, said to me one day, "I'm bin out here all this time, now you come back out and you got a nice car, jewelry and bikes..." It did Look that way, but he didn't see that all night of hustling I was doing, and some nights were so quiet, you wonder why you do it... Some time passed, and money on the streets was real slow, but I knew it would pass, I just had to ride the slow wave a sec... Now since I had purchased my car, I would get it cleaned every day, pay a guy $40, to clean the inside and outside... So, when my boys saw me cleaning my car myself, they wondered why, because I would never clean my own car... I told them, "Money is Low..." Had to keep it real...

On Parole side of things... I had told my P.O. that I switched jobs and now I worked on the Hussle Truck... It was a government program to give people work and they got paid weekly... My cousin Renee Darrell was the Supervisor of one of the work trucks they sent out daily... You would meet at the Hussle truck office, and go in the trucks to different locations/ areas and clean up or cut grass... It was actually a good way for people to earn money... Even though my money was low, I couldn't bring myself to actually work on it... I was in new clothes every day, and a fresh car... Couldn't degrade myself like that... I was too proud/ too good, to do that job... That's how I thought at the time...

Since my cousin was a manager, I told her if my P.O. calls, just say I work on your truck and you pay me in cash... I had told her this a few months ago... So, one day I go to my regular schedule meeting... As soon as the meeting starts, my P.O. asked me, "How is work??" I didn't think nothing of it, it was summer time, so I said, "Work is cool, it's hot out there working though…" He replies, "O ok, well I went to the Hustle Truck Offices, to Look for You, and they said, "They Have Not heard of No Gernel Darrell!!!" My Heart Dropped, and I started to think Fast… I said, "No Way, I'm been Working!!!" Then I said instantly, "Are you sure you said Gernel Darrell??" He said, "Yes…" I replied, "My cousin is my Supervisor, you could call her now… I'm bin working…" I pull out my phone to get her number… Now I'm thinking, "I hope she remembers that I told her to say I work for her!!!" I give the number to him and he calls her…

When he calls her, I can hear her through the phone, but he doesn't know that she is loud enough that I also hear the conversation… He says, "This is Parole Officer, Mr M., and I'm calling because I have a Gernel Darrell here that CLAIMS, he works with you on the hustle truck…" She says, "NO, He Don't Work for Me…" I'm thinking, "O GOD!!!" He said, "Are you sure??" She says, "Yes…" It was a pause… Then she says, "Gernel Darrell, O, yes, he does work on my truck…" So, he asks her, "How does he get paid??" She replied, "In cash…" He then says, "Ok and thank you…" To her and hangs up the phone… Then he says to me, "Ok, you escape, she said you work with her…" I said, "See!!!" As to say, I told you so… And we left it as that, as far as the conversation about work…

Fuck, I was Nervous!!! When I got out the meeting, I went and saw my mom and told her the story… She said, "That was close TUB!!! Maybe you should go work on the hustle truck then??" I replied, "No way, Fuck that!!!" (working on that truck) But yes, that was a close call though!!!" A month or 2 later, I did join the hustle truck for a bit... My money was super low, and I had to get it back up... When I had enough money to sustain my lifestyle again, I just didn't sign back up... So, I worked on the truck for a month or two and then, I was back to my Vacation...

Things were going Good again, so I decided one day when visiting my P.O... That I'll show him how I filled out an application form... One of my ace girls convinced me to fill out an application for some company... So, at the visit, I said to him, "See, I'm trying to get a decent job..." Because after our incident when he went look for me at the Hustle Truck, and they said they don't know me... He complained that the hustle truck wasn't a Legit Job...

I used to say, how could it not be legit, it's Government, and they pay good... Well, you were getting $500 a week, and that wasn't bad for average pay... But they didn't have insurance and all, it was just like a good paying hustle... I wasn't on the hustle truck anyway, except for a month or 2, but that was my cover for my Full-Time Vacation I was on... My P.O. says, "O, nice... Since you are looking, for a job, I have some people at Butterfield and Vallis, and they are Hiring..." My Heart dropped, this can't be true!!! I was just Bull-Shitting, I didn't want a job!!! But I couldn't tell my P.O. this... One of my rules was, I HAD to Work...

He proceeded to pick up the phone and make a call... He spoke to his peoples, and I had an interview the same day... We would meet at 11am and the interview was later that day at 2pm... "WTF!!!" (What the Fuck), I thought to myself, "You, stupid ass, acting all cocky, has ended your Vacation!!!" Obviously, I had to go to the interview... And just my luck, this place was a ware-house distributor (business) and they liked to give, X addicts, or X prisoners a chance at Legit Life... I think they just like the cheap labour, and having you by the balls, because this was like one of the only places that gave people with a troubled past, a chance... Because most places probably won't give a x prisoner a chance, especially if the person/ guy went jail for stealing... I didn't have no stealing shit on my record, just the other shit, but either way, just my damn Luck, they hired me...

The job was cool though, met a few nice people... The pay was shit... I made like $430 a week, that's 5 days a week, starting at 7am to like 5pm... At first, I just dealt with it, because the P.O. was still in tune with the whole process... Once he knew I was settled in, he backed off a little... Then I decided with the pay they give me, it's not worth it... I would have to deliver all sorts of shit to restaurants, bars, and businesses... Big slabs of meat, vegetables, and everything under the sun, and you had to carry that shit upstairs sometimes... And I was still hustling on the side, and on a good day you could make $400 in the streets, so I started to go work when I felt like it... But before I did this, I tried to see if I did overtime, could I raise the, sum of money coming in from the job... And even with over time, the pay was still ridiculous... So not only did I attend work when I Felt like it, I would also be late, and also don't call when I'm not coming in...

The Boss soon got tired of all this, and fired me one day... I had been pre-warned to straighten up my act with warnings, written warnings and all... So, when he called me to his office and fired me, I tried to plead for my job, because I knew my P.O. won't be happy... I said to the Boss, "I thought you said this place is about second chances and helping people…" They had like a counselling service they sent people on drugs before they fired them… I tried to get the Boss send me there, and not fire me… He wasn't hearing none of it… I was Done/ Fired…

I got up, went to my locker and cleared it out, and walked out the building to my bike… I thought to myself, "What am I going to tell the P.O.??" And then I thought, "Thank God, you Free from that place!!!" I had been there like 7 or so long months of working there… Then I thought, "I wonder if he will call my P.O. and tell him I got fired?? Because I definitely wasn't telling him…" And I jumped on my bike and headed to my neighbourhood to see what the day brings…

It felt Good to be back on Vacation… But I was still a little worried, would the Boss call the P.O…

I was lucky, the Boss never told my P.O. and neither did I… So, I just went on as I was still working with the company, whenever we had meetings, and he asked about work… As I reflect back on the job, I remember I have never been so scared in my Life… I was a Truck Helper basically, so they would send me out with a driver for the day… They would put me with a real cool guy, I can't remember his name… I had gone out with many drivers, but he stands out and was the scariest time because, this guy liked Heroine…(Dope/Brown) He was always High, which I didn't really mind, because I'm from the streets, so I had been used to being around High people… Now Dope is a drug, and it gets people so high, where they can hardly stay awake… They go in a Dreamy like state, and want to just close their eyes… I had been used to being around someone that was high on dope… But having someone drive you that

High on Dope, is a whole another level!!! And to make it worst, we were in this big ass delivery Truck, that have the refrigerated backs...

We would be driving, and he would be talking to me, and next second, he gone quiet... I don't think nothing of it, until I see the truck swerve a little/ cross the yellow line, and I look at him, and he basically going sleep at the wheel... I immediately call his name... This fucker snaps out of it, eyes pop back open, and he continues exactly where he left off on whatever he was saying... I think to myself, "Ain't/ Isn't this some shit!!! He doesn't even realise he was just going sleep!!! He going to Kill Me for sure!!!" From that point on, I kept a close eye on him... If he blinked too long, I'll be like, "You Awake??"

I knew it was Dope he was using, because that would be the first stop we make most mornings... We would load up the truck with our deliveries for the day, and the first Stop we made when we left the yard, was to the Pusher-Man, Drug dealers house/ spot, so he (the driver) could get his shit... I liked the guy, but working with him was hard... I couldn't go to the Boss and say, "Look, I think I'm going to Die, the fucking driver getting too high..." Number 1, drugs were against work rules, and 2, I'm from the streets, so you don't tell on your own, or tell on anyone period...

Bermuda roads are small as it is, so I was sure we would crash in that truck one day, but Thank God, we didn't crash, and I finally got changed to another driver, or I got fired or something... It was a good learning experience though... Not only did I take the knowledge of the ware house and how they work it, and delivery work knowledge away from the job with me… But after that, I vowed never to get "Fired" from a Job again!!! It be better to say to my P.O., "I Quit, instead of, I Got Fired…" But it was all good, Life goes on…

As time went on, my Money started to get low again… So, my mom linked me with a lady she used to work with, and she gave me a job up at the New New-Stead Hotel… I was to be a House-Men… This worked out fine at first… Well the only issue I had the whole time I was there, was making my time to work… I was still in Party mode… So, trying to get work on time, after a night out of drinking, didn't work out too Good… But my work was excellent… One day the Boss Lady would be praising me saying, "You're such a good worker…" And then the next time I was late, she would jump on me hard… This time in particular, I understood, and try to show her how, I hadn't been late for a minute/ little while, and I have gotten a bit better with my time… She proceeds to tell me, "If I'm late again, I will get one last warning, and the next time I'll be fired!!!"

I had been there for 6 or more months… But I knew I'll be late again, and I knew I'll eventually get fired… But I said to myself, I'll just try hard and make my time… Shit, it was probably a week later, and here I was Late again… I knew I had Fucked up… You know when u get in one of them moods, you know you fucked up, and don't want someone keep telling you… Well I go into work, I was only 15minutes late, and the Boss lady was making off… I say, "I understand, I messed up, but it was an honest mistake this time…" I don't think I was out partying, but either way, I was still late… I did have to travel over 10 plus miles to work, and the island of Bermuda 24 square miles… So, it could have been traffic, an accident, anything…

She doesn't want to hear None of it… Maybe she had a long night, she was severely overweight… She was saying, "I should Fire you right now!!!" I said, "You said I still have one chance…" She replied, "She didn't care, and how bad of a worker I am…" I said, "Last week you had me cleaning front desk area, and telling me how good it is, and now you are saying this…" After she finished with the threats of how she should fire me, she let me go off to work… If I didn't get nothing from these jobs, I always take the knowledge of it, and I always seem to meet some nice people… When I leave her office, I go to the other house man guy, and I say, "I'm going to Quit…" He understood… I said, "If I don't, I'm going to get Fired soon for sure…" Him and a next maid lady, I was cool with… I went to her next, and told her my thoughts… She tried to talk me out of it, but my mind was made up…

I walked back into the Boss's office… I said to her, "My Services are no longer needed here, I think I'm going to have to let myself go… I Quit!!!" And then I turned around and walked out the office and straight to my car and left…My P.O. knew I had switched jobs and was working here at Newstead now… He would come up to the job for our weekly brief visits, so I don't have to go in to his office to see him… And the more he had seen me in the New Stead uniform the more trust I gained from him… I'll just tell him I'm off from work, so I'll come to his office for the visit, so he doesn't know I quit my job… I'll work it out… I Always Do…

GERNEL L. DARRELL

...CHAPTER 4...
...Meeting the Parole Board/Jobs...

$\mathcal{P}$arole was going ok, I was surviving, working my way around it, so I can stay on Vacation... It's not that I didn't want to work, well that wasn't Fully the reason, I felt like being "Behind Bars" was like being in War, it was Hard Work to Survive, Mentally... And I had basically worked most of my time in jail... So, I felt I needed a long vacation, even though it was mandatory, (A must) that I must work, since they released me on parole... I always fronted, (acted) like I was employed, so they would stay off my back... And all you needed was a good cover job, and someone the P.O. could call to confirm... Also get a letter typed and signed to say how much hours you work and your weekly pay... A little more to it but that was it basically...

It was all about Trust... You had to know how to get your P.O. to Trust You... When I met with him, even though I wasn't working... I'll say work is good, and give a quick little work story... (All made up) And then I tell him some real problems I'm having, in a relationship or family or whatever, and then I'll ask for his advice... Guess it makes them feel good, when you act like you need their help... All the while I'm just keeping his/ their mind off the Job shit, because the parole board won't like the idea of me not working...

I had them figured out… I thought to myself, "After 5 years of Jail, and scheming inside, I could handle pulling the wool over one person's eyes…" In jail you had multiple people you got to be able to get over, in authority figures I mean… The officers watched you, and could search or piss test you, at any time/ randomly… Especially if you looked like you high on drugs… When I was inside and in their drug program, I was smoking weed, so you had to get someone who was not using substances to piss in a little bottle, so you could dummy the test and pass it… Because they tested you every week in that program… The clean piss/ urine was easy to find most times for me, if it was an emergency, you pay someone, and you'll get it instantly… You had to be on guard, they would call you to the office, and "bang surprise test…" I stayed prepared or just said, I can't go/ use the bathroom… I wasn't looked at as a threat, they looked at me like a Good boy, and that's what I Wanted/ Needed…

So, basically, I was pretty much On Top, of my shit, until I made a Very Big Mistake!!! This day, I'm out the road, Court Street and it's evening time… Me and my cousin Snoop are standing there on the side of the street, drinking Nips, (miniatures bottles) of Vodka and Guinness… My cousin is called Snoop, because he was slim like Snoop Dogg, same skin colour and all, and my cousin's hair used to be long and he had good hair, so it looked like when the rapper Snoop Dogg had his Perm… My cousin was into music also, and liked to perform on stage shows… Always would also be in Chew-Stick… Chew-stick was an Open Mike bar, and you could go on stage and do poetry or whatever…

My cousin Snoop, was Pretty Good also, he could Rap, DJ Reggae and even Sing… He was my first cousin, and we grew up tight from young… He wasn't as Wild as me, when it came to fights and shit, but he was down for me 100% never the less… So, this day as we are chilling, and just drinking, so we decided to take my convertible town to the bar… My White Renault soft top Convertible… Looking Clean as always… I put down the roof, turn up the music loud and we head to Captains Club in town, to get a drink and see what girls are up in there…

We get town and park… I leave the top down like a BOSS, of course, and I had parked directly in front of the club door… It's not a parking bay, but it after work hours, so you didn't really have to worry about parking tickets, so I would park where ever I felt like it… We get up in the Club called Captains, it's a good vibe, girls at the bar, plus I'm got loot(money) in my pocket… Me and Snoop, drinking, taking shots… I'm buying drinks for girls that I think are cute… And talking to which ever one I want…

If I was in a bar and drinking, I could easily make conversation with any girl I wanted… Guess it was the liquid confidence alcohol gives you… We finally leave, I think I got a few new numbers from the girls I had met during the night… The bar also had a dance floor and DJ, so it was always an ok vibe… We head out in my car, and I say I'll go to the 24/7 gas station… Which at this time it was the only one, (gas station) that stayed open late/ all night…

After we stopped gas station, we were going to head back out to the streets or to the hood… But maybe the streets I thought, because it was late, and the hood be too quiet… So, I pull into the gas station and the police are parked up sitting there like they always are, I pay them no mind, like usual… I

GERNEL L. DARRELL

go in store and see this fat girl from the hood... I must have been drunk, because I was saying some sly shit to her... She was in a jeep outside the store entrance... I went in the gas station and got food, and went back to my car and drove out...

I'm driving down the road, and say to Snoop, "I forgot to get gas, I'm going back..." He said, "Don't go back!!!" He saw the Police there... I'm bull/ hard headed... I needed gas, plus once we got back where we were going, I was going to try and go see a chick I was chatting to on line... (on my cell phone) I go back and get gas, pay and then leave... This time when I leave the police pull out behind me, and flash their lights for me to stop... I pull over, and the cop gets out and walks up to my window and asks for my license...

I usually keep my license in the little slot right next to the steering wheel, where the cd player area is... But it wasn't there... I checked a next spot, and it wasn't there either... I said to the cop, "I can't find it..." In my mind, it just seemed like too much to look for it... Guess it was all the alcohol...

He tells me get out the car and asked if I had been drinking... I said 2 Guinness I guess... He breathed test me, and I was handcuffed and put in the back of a patrol car... The next step was, I would be taken to the Police Station to JAIL... This broke my heart, knowing I had Fucked Up, on such a Big level... I was going to be taken off the road, My P.O. going be mad, and now I'm on my back to behind Bars!!! This was a Sad Night!!! I thought to myself, why you just didn't listen, and not go back and get gas!!!

But when I look at it on a Whole... What was I expecting to happen?? I was partying Everyday... And Driving... And when me and Logy, would go West and party… (Town guys couldn't go West and party, they would literally get shot/killed, but we guys were Good anywhere we went) After a long night of drinking with all the west guys… We would literally race, my car with a little red car Logy had brought for his mom… Logy be in the car with me, and LOGY's cousin Mad Ed would drive the little red one… So, if Ed was there we would race the 2 cars all the way town, to the central part of the island… And sometimes all the way East to the other end of the island, to party more… That was High Speed Racing… I'll be driving my car of course, with my top down… Ed was a driver, so we would battle hard the whole way… And that be after drinking Chivas alcohol all night… Shot after shot…

But anyway, here I was Off to Jail!!! I couldn't believe it!!! When I got there, I was like double or more, over the legal limit of alcohol, that you were allowed by Law, to have in your system when you drive… For instance, if it was 80 percent legal limit I was like 230… They booked me and put me into a cell… I just laid down and try to sleep… Next thing I know they come cross asking if I want breakfast, but I decline their food… I tell them, "Let me Leave!!! Fuck, I'm been Booked, I Want to Go!!!"

The Realization of it All, is dawning on me… I guess the alcohol was wearing off… And all I want is out this Fucking Cell!!! I'm banging on the cell door, to someone comes… With my foot, arm, anything to make some noise… Of course, I'm not hurting myself, but I'm losing my Damn Mind!!! I want Out, Now!!! I'm thinking if they don't let me Go Now, I'm going to Attack, the first officer that Opens this cell… I was going Crazy!!!

GERNEL L. DARRELL

Then I thought, "No, Don't Do that!!! Then you definitely won't be freed... They finally came and took me back to the breath test and said, "We can't let you go, until the machine says your sober..." I was still about double over the level, I was Mad!!! I couldn't believe this shit... Before I went Prison, I had a few DUI's and they usually just let me go the next morning... Except on occasions when it was a Friday night and holiday Monday, I'll have to stay in that cell to I went court on Tuesday... They suggested I should eat the shitty microwave dinner or lunch they made for the prisoners, to help my alcohol level drop... I ate it, in hopes my alcohol level would drop faster...

The whole time I Can't Believe, I'm Sitting in a Mother-Fucking Cell!!! My Mind was all over the place... Them fuckers finally let me go... They had drove my car to the police garage, and let my cousin walk free that night... It felt Good to be Free again, but I knew they would take me off the road... My first order of business, was to go get my car... I just had to get a lift to the police compound to get the car, they didn't make me pay for it... I get my car and head home, and then to the hood, to find my cousin Snoop and tell him what happened... When I reach my cousin the first thing he says is, "I told you don't go back for gas..."

Next, I get a call from my P.O., he knows already about the D.U.I... (Driving Under the influence) He wants to meet me Immediately... I go visit him... At the visit, he isn't happy about me getting in trouble, and to make matters worse... He had finally heard about me leaving the job up New Stead Hotel... I just said the Job wasn't working out for me, so I went back on the Hustle Truck as work... So, this was also an Issue, and now the DUI...

60

He asked me what happened with the DUI?? I said, "I was celebrating my Baby's First Christmas, (I guess it was around that time) and I just had a few drinks, I wasn't drunk..." Well he gave me a paper, it said that, "I will be seeing the Parole Board, for the offence I committed, and not following the rule of a Full Time Job, because he feels the hustle truck is not suitable... This was the WORST of the WORST!!! Yes, it was already bad, that'll be taken off the road, and fined heavily, but the Parole Board was Bad, Bad!!!

These people, the Parole Board could send me back WESTGATE to Jail!!! They had the power to Revoke, my Parole... Basically they could take away my Freedom!!! And return me to Prison!!! And I'll be basically, Dead!!! I knew I "Couldn't Handle It" being locked back up... I mean if there was no other choice, ok, but NO, that couldn't happen, I Hoped... On the letter he gave me, I looked at the date of when I'll be seeing the Parole Board... I would be seeing the Parole Board in about 3 weeks... This was not good... I could lose my freedom in 3 weeks...

On the day I saw the parole board, I was to go to the Prison's Headquarters Building for the meeting... When I arrived there my P.O. was already there... I had to get a lift to the meeting because I had already been to court, and the judge took me off the road for a year, and fined me... This day of the meeting was a Scary Day... Ever since the DUI, I had been telling my mom, I think they going to lock me back up... I knew my P.O. didn't really care, so I couldn't get no help from him... It all depended on how this meeting went... My mom asked if I want her come up and try talk to the parole board... I think I said yes come... Also, if they sent me jail, I wanted her there, so she would know I'm gone, one time…

I decided to wait outside the building until it was time to see the board… There was a next guy who came and was waiting to see the Parole Board also, so we chatted while we waited… When he came, he was riding on a mountain/ push bike, and stashed it behind a bush, in the yard… He was cool, he told me how he was also on Parole and has the same P.O. as me… He said, he hasn't been working, and he caught a Case, for having Counterfeit Money, but he should get off … (the case) But he said they (the parole board) shouldn't Revoke/ take his Parole away, and send him back jail because of the working issue… I agreed… I didn't really care, I was just listening to the story and wondering what they will do with me…

They finally called us inside, because they were ready to proceed (start)… My mom had arrived, and she waited in the sitting area until my P.O. will call her to have a chance to speak to the Parole Board, when time… They had us wait outside the room the meeting will be held in… And this when it all started becoming more real… For us to go into the meeting we had to be escorted in like how we were when we were in jail… 2 officers on each side of you… The other guy went in to see the Parole Board first, and I sat in a chair outside in the quiet hall and just listened…

I can hear what's going on inside the meeting… The guy I was just talking to outside is pleading his case, but someone from the Parole Board is saying, "Your Parole officer is saying, you ain't/ are not showing up to your meetings, and you are not working…" He was saying, he got laid off/ let go because work was slow, and he was having a hard time trying to find more work... I was thinking he is taking the wrong approach, by saying he having a hard time finding work... They ain't/ are not going to want to hear that... He then said, the P.O. outside, which he was talking about where I was sitting... The P.O. was standing close to where I was sitting so I knew he heard, what was going on...

The guy was trying to tell the Parole Board to call his Parole Officer, into the room to confirm that, whenever he didn't show up for a meeting, he called him to let him know... The Parole Board was not hearing None of it... I guess the P.O. and the Parole Board already knew the outcome of his meeting... The Parole Board told him, "His Parole is REVOKED, and he is being RECALLED/ Sent Back to JAIL, Immediately!!!"

Do Not pass GO! Do Not collect $200! Go directly to Jail!!! Just like the game Monopoly... He was Gone, and it was Nothing he could do... He came out the room in Tears, and the officers were holding him, and he said to the P.O., "Why you tell them I didn't call or showed up??" I guess he wanted answers... The P.O. just looked at him, and didn't reply... Before another word could be spoken, the officers hand cuffed him... He was trying to say, "You don't have to put cuffs on me..." Next, they start to lead him down the hall and away to the waiting prison van to take him back to jail... He was trying to say wait, wait, because he was talking to his P.O., but they weren't hearing it... They just dragged/ muscled him away... His judgment was read by the Parole Board and he was Prison's Property Now!!!

I'm thinking what the Fuck, just like that he was heading back to jail... Could this be my fate also?? Well we will see...

My P.O. went in first to speak to the board, I guess to up-date them and tell them his thoughts on me… I couldn't hear what was going on, it was much quieter than when, the other guy was in there… My P.O. came out and then he went get my mom and she got her chance to chat with the Parole board… And now it was my time to face the Parole Board… Before I can enter the room, 2 Prison officers come and escort me in the room, one on my left and one on my right… As I walk into the room, it's a big table with one chair on one side for me, and the Parole Board was sitting on the other side… At least 8 of them I guess…

They proceed and get straight to the point, and say, "We have 2 issues on hand…. 1, An offence of DUI… And 2, you are not working fully, and both are Violations of your Release Rules!!! So why shouldn't We, The Parole Board, Re-call you, or Revoke your Parole?? (Send you back jail basically) My Heart and Mind start Racing!!! I thought about their questions, I thought about how I used to be the one who set up for these meetings, when they had to see people in jail and decide if they would release them or not, because I was the Administrative Cleaner, in Jail… And that was one of my duties, to set up the meeting area and break it down… Up jail the kitchen would make sandwiches and cookies, and cut up fruit for them… And I had to do all the setting up and display, and get coffee and tea urns set up… That was all before I got caught with my cell phone… All of that happened in jail of course…

But all that was far behind me now, and if I didn't answer properly, I'll be back to square one!!! (in jail) So, I replied, as Soft and as Nicely and as Ass Kissing as I could, so I could sound Sincere and also still seem like myself, because they weren't stupid... And with 8 of them, one might see through me if I wasn't on point... But this wasn't No Joke, and I Knew it... I Couldn't fail in my mind, because if I did, I'll get taken away just like that other guy... All these thoughts went through my mind so quick... I even thought about how I would jump out a window, if they said I'm got to go back jail... I had the route already planned... It was a window right outside this door, and they would take me out there and hand cuff me... But as soon as we open that door, Ill dive right out the window, and run for it... I had to Focus!!!

You would have thought I was a computer searching through my data base, for a solution for a problem... So, I replied, talking kind of fast and Pleadingly... I said, "I have been working, I work on the Hussle Truck... The P.O. feels it's not a Suitable Job because they have No Insurance, so that's where we had an issue..." I went on... "Since he had an issue with it, I'm been looking around and working with him to find something suitable..." I paused, then went again... "But I say, he feels it's not suitable, but we make good money on there, and it's a good job..." They did make ok money, $500 something for 5 days of work, and you were only cleaning, or cutting grass, or whatever they chose, or had on for the day... Where at Butterfield-n-Vallis, you make $430 a week and you start early and break your back...

I didn't say all that to them though... I continued, "And on the matter of the D.U.I... I had just had a few drinks, because I was celebrating that I had my First child, and it was Our First Christmas together..." I said, "I usually don't drink At All!!!" It was a woman on the board, she was the first woman Premier, she says, "So when you go dinner, you don't drink??" I said, "Maybe one or 2 glasses of wine, but I'm into fitness, I stay away from Alcohol…" She replies, "Do you know that, you are NOT ALLOWED to Drink?? You signed your Parole form, that says No Drinking…" I said, "I didn't know, I was not allowed to drink At All…" and I also said, "It didn't say, No Drinking on my form, I Would have saw that…"

She hands my parole papers/ forms in my direction, and one of the officers grabs it and hands it to me… She says, "Section 2 or whatever, and tells me to read it out loud…" I read it… Basically it said… "You(I) are not allowed to be in control of any illegal substances, or under the influence of any illegal substances…" Then she pointed out another section that says, "I am not allowed to break ANY LAW, At All…" I say, "Well, I didn't know they meant Alcohol… I thought they meant Anything Illegal, and Alcohol isn't Illegal…" I was trying to use that as my defence now, that I didn't know I could drink at All… I knew NOW though… She replied, "No you are not allowed to drink At All!!! And you can't even Litter!!! Any Law Broken, can make you Violate your Parole…" I dipped my head like a scolded puppy and said, "Ok, I understand, but I didn't know…"

They told me to step out of the meeting, so they could make their decision… The P.O. was still out there… I sat back in my same seat, and looking to see if I can actually escape, if they say Jail… The window was right here, and Open… I thought push come-to-shove, maybe I could dive out the window, to get out quick and run… The drop wasn't that high… It'll be better than jail… I didn't say nothing to the P.O., I just sat there quiet… He tried to make small talk, but nah, I wasn't entertaining him… I just sat there with my thoughts… They called for me to return back into the room, about 5 to 10 mins later…

I walk back into the room and sit down… The officers are still on my sides… I wasn't used to all this officer shit, not since I'm been free, so it felt like jail already… A man on the Parole Board asks one time, "About this Working… How soon can you get a Full-time job??" From the question, I knew they wasn't going to send me back jail/ lock me back up, but I knew I wasn't out the Hot water just yet… I replied, "I will have a job in one month, I Promise you that!!!" Then they say, "About this other matter… Don't you think, since Alcohol/ drinking was involved in your initial crime… Do you think you have a problem with Alcohol??" I say, "No because I didn't really drink before, and now I know I can't drink, we'll Not Allowed, because of Parole… I definitely, Will Not Touch Any Alcohol!!!" They replied, "Well we think you should take a Treatment Course, and your P.O. will have the info… You Must Attend it!!!" I replied, "I don't think I need to, but I'll definitely attend and do what's got to be done…" And I thanked them for the chance and for not Revoking My Parole/ Recall me… They said, "They will see me in a month's time, and I better have full time employment!!!" I was escorted out the meeting… I told my P.O., I have a month to get a full-time job, and we agreed on our next meeting date, and I was Free to Leave…

I stepped outside and took a breath of fresh air… That was all too close for comfort, I must get a job For-Real this time… Them people would definitely Lock me up, and won't even care… I thought about the guy that's going back jail… And then I thought about his push bike he left behind the bushes… I went and looked at it… It was a Nice and

New bike 2... I thought to myself, "He won't be needing this bike, he on his way back Jail!!!" And I was off the road, so this bike is coming with me!!! It could be my new Wheels... So, I got on it, and rode it off the Prison Headquarters yard, and headed home, to Start Looking for a Job...

...CHAPTER 5...
...OFF the ROAD/ WORK...

I had a month to find suitable employment, or I could be in Big trouble and wind back up in jail... My ways of having a Front/ Pretend job, won't work on this occasion... The Parole board was on me this time... I was looking all around and filling out applications, for any type of work/ job... I had my high school papers and that's was the only thing you really needed... But now I had a Criminal record, and I had to tell the people about it at the job interviews... I was going to lots of interviews, and I had my resume done up and ready... I wasn't having no Luck...

Two weeks later, I got a job with a Landscaping Company, that my boy Fab, used to work for... He called them and gave a good word about me, so they gave me a chance... The job was cool, I started like 6am, and finish like 6pm... That was bullshit, and the pay was low... You made like $380 for your 5day work week, but I didn't care... I had a Legit job, with insurance, and the Parole board can't say shit... I think the pay was so low, because they employed a lot of foreigners, and they didn't mind the lower pay... They knew the value of what they were making and worked with it... This job I learned all about gardening and planting trees... Well enough to get by, because I wasn't into the shit like that...

I also had signed up for the treatment that the Parole board requested... I had to go down to the old St. Brendan's Mental Hospital building, which is now called the Mid-Atlantic Wellness Institute... When I met with the new guy/ counsellor at the treatment place they sent me, I told him the reason I'm here to meet him and take his drug/drink counselling/ monitoring... I Down Played the whole situation... The way I told him the story, I played it like I never drink, and I'm into fitness, and it was a one-time thing... So instead of him putting me in a treatment group class... I would just have to come and meet him once a week... And when we meet, I'll be tested for alcohol and everything and we will just leave it as the meetings for now...

I agreed, another meeting won't kill me... I knew they won't be able to really test your piss for Alcohol... They probably have the technology now, but I knew back then they didn't... I knew the in's and out's, of the test... When I was in jail and working in medical, I would steal the piss test, so I could test myself also... I also used to give the test to my boys/ mates, so they could make sure they don't get caught with dirty urine either... But yes, I agree with this new counsellor I had met, whatever he said was cool with me...

A month later it was time to have the follow up, meeting with the Parole board again... I went to the meeting in my work uniform, not just to show them, but because I had to leave work and go to the meeting... This meeting was a little more relaxed, I didn't have to worry, if I'll be sent back jail because I had done all they asked... I went to the Prison headquarters building and waited to the Parole Board was, ready to see me... When they met with me and saw the uniform, it confirmed I had got a decent job like they requested... They also saw the notes from my P.O. to say I did what was asked of me, as far as going to the treatment center... So, they told me "Stay out of Trouble" and let me leave... THANK GOD, all that meeting the parole board shit was All Over!!!

My job wasn't that far from my mom's house... My mom moved from court street and moved back closer to my Hood, Middle Town...(M-Town) So, I would leave there like 5:30am, jump on the same push-bike, that I got a month ago from outside the prison headquarters, at my first meeting... And I'll just ride work... I hated this job, especially getting up so early, to go rush around from yard to yard and cut grass... My Precious car, was parked outside my mom's house, so every morning I'll look at my car and wish I could drive it... I don't talk about my daughter much in this book, but she was also a big part of my world, if not My Whole World!!! I always made sure I spent loads of time with her... She such an Angel... So, between her, work and Everyday Life, I was just chilling...

I wasn't partying as much, because I was off the road, and Logy was locked back up, for whatever reason... Work, starting early and finishing late kept me tired... I was dealing with it, but I was growing tired of this Slave Work!!! I wondered, how long will this job last/ How long will I put up with it... Time went by and it probably lasted 6 months to a year, maybe more... Then I got fed up with the job, so I Quit... I would just find another job... This time I told my P.O., I wasn't trying to let him find out on his own... He didn't make too much fuss which surprised me a little... I just guaranteed I'll find something more suitable for me soon… I think he liked the idea that I was trying to be honest with him…

But I wasn't no fool, I had seen and talked to other guys on Parole, and others that had the same guy as me for their Parole Officer… This P.O. was No Joke, he had sent at least 8 guys to the Parole board, that had been sent back to jail, in one year… I think it was because he was from Canada, and people all over the island were losing their jobs… So, he wanted to show the system/ parole board that he was a good worker for them and he was needed… So, guys feared him as a P.O.…. I just knew you had to stay on, Top of your Game, because if he caught you slipping, to the parole board you go… So, I immediately went back looking for a job…

I got an interview for a Kitchen Porter Job, at White Horse in St, Georges… The interview was with the Head-Chef and the Manager or Owner… I can't remember who exactly, the other guy was, buy they were 2 white males… They both seemed like nice guys and were feeling/ liked my vibe… I told them about my conviction and that I was on Parole… They seemed more Amazed at the story if anything… The Head Chef was a cool guy, he said the pay be $10 an hour and it's an On-Call Job, and the work schedules will be done up later… He also said, if I didn't mind the pay, I seem like a cool enough guy, even though I'm on Parole, he will hire me… Now the pay was the lowest I'm ever heard of… That cheap American wages or 3rd World Country shit Pay… Before I went jail I was getting like between $24 and $28 an hour… I Really, needed a job though, My P.O. wasn't No Joke!!!

I agreed I'll take the pay and be on call, but my conditions for excepting it were… I told him, I needed a letter for my

P.O. that says I'm Hired and I'll be working 40 hours a week and the pay rate… He said no problem, he will call me when my letter done/ ready… Ok, it was settled… That ended up being a good interview and I walked out with the Job and my Urgently Needed letter was coming…

He called me a week later, and he had my letter that I Needed, for my P.O., and I also got the schedule for work at the same time… The schedule said, I was to go in to work on Sundays, from 6pm to 12… That was great for me, one day a week, and my letter for P.O. says 40 hours of work a week… So, my P.O. can't say shit… The letter didn't state all the details of the schedule, it just said I'm hired and I'll be working 40 hours a week pretty much… The Chef/ Manager signed it and all…

So basically, I was back on Vacation, except for my 2 meetings, and one day of work… I was still off the road though… So, I decided to take a 12week program, that if you pay $300, you could do this, Driver Awareness Course, and get 3 months off your time, that you have, off the road… So, I'll be off the road for 9 months instead of 12 months… I done the course and waited because once u have 3 months left, you go back court and tell the judge you done the course, and the judge re-instates you/ gives u back your license…

During my time off the road, I met many female friends… One worth mentioning was a Portuguese girl, that I met outside Social Club Bar, one day… I mention her because, she had a car license, and could drive a stick shift car, so I decided to let her be my driver… That was a relief, to be able to still go around in my car… A few months later, the car went off the road, and I still had a long time left off the road, so I parked it back in front of my mom's house again... Soon after that me and the Portuguese girl stopped being cool, for whatever reason... Then I met a next cutie/ girl... This girl really liked my company and had a bike, so I would let her ride me/ tow me/ be my rider for where ever I wanted to go... So even though I was off the road, I was still getting around a bit...

The job at White Horse was convenient, no money really, but I was hustling on the side anyway... Trying to sell some shit/ drugs in the streets at night, and only having to work on Sundays... As easy as the White Horse Job was, and convenient as it was, I soon grew tired of even travelling, St. Georges, to go to the work place on Sunday... I wasn't back on the road yet, so I had to find a ride there... I would say Fuck it, and not even go to work...

I was making $70 something each time I went to the job on Sunday... I would be there for about 7 or 8 hours... This was no money for me, so I decided to Quit... I knew he wouldn't call my P.O., and me and the P.O. was cool now... I had gained back his trust... I had been out of jail for around 4 years now, and I had another 4 to go...

At the end of 9 months, I returned to Court, and the judge acknowledges the Driving Awareness Class I took, and gives me back my license/ puts me back on the road... I immediately, get my car ready, so I can start Driving Again...

...CHAPTER 6...
...NO DISRESPECT / FIGHTS....

A lot has been going on, but I was managing to stay out of Jail... Now during this 4 years, other than relationship drama, I managed to get into 3 Real fights... Well 2, was somewhat fights, and the third I had to use a Machete... Well I didn't have to, but I did... I'll start with the first incident...

At this point, I can't remember if I was working one of my many jobs I had, or when I was on my so-called vacation, but this was when I had my First P.O... I had ridden/ rode my bike, up Warwick to J.V.C. (Jones's Village) to go visit my good brethren, that's like my brother, JAHNI... We had met during my first years in jail and now we both were out... He was Free, and I was on Parole... He wasn't just my boy, he was my connect at the time... I trusted him, and like to fuck with people I could trust... So, I was chilling in his hood and waiting for him to get back/ return...

My phone rings and I answer... It's my cousin Snoop... Now Snoop has a younger brother Matthew, who I Love Dearly... When I was in jail, Matthew was training to be a Boxer... He would always say to me, his Big cousin (this was before I went jail) that he thinks he could beat me in a fight... I would just laugh at his little ass... He was taller than me a little, but No Way in hell was I letting him beat me… Shit, the biggest guy couldn't beat me, I thought… Plus he didn't have the Heart to go the distance, for a real fight I mean… I could see right through his act… But he was good at boxing…

One day when Matthew was boxing training and running on the beach… After his run, he must have decided to go for a swim in the ocean… He runs into the water and tries to Dive in/ under the water too early… His head hit the ground, and he was automatically knocked out… People on the beach had to run in the water, to save him and drag him out the water and call the ambulance… When he woke, he would never walk again… Must have broken his spine or neck…

So, Matthew is in a wheel chair now, and all his friends must have stayed close to him when it first happened, but now no one really cares for him… Not even our own cousins look out for him anymore, and we guys were all tight… Since I saw this when I came out of jail, I made it my Goal to try look out for him often… I would always go looking for him and find him at the dock fishing… It was either, ALBUOY's Point Dock or Riddles Bay Dock… He would be there sitting in his wheel chair and fishing rod in hand, and be so Happy I had come by to check on him…

The first thing he always done was open the cooler, that he always had next to him, and show me all the Big Fish he had caught… The sizes of the fish always surprised me, because at that time it was bigger than any fish I had ever caught… A few times when I was there chilling and talking with him, he would get a fish on his rod… He'll be saying to me, "I think I'm got him…" And when he realizes, he does have the fish hooked, and the fish is pulling the rod fighting to get away…

He would say, "TUB hold the Chair!!!(wheelchair) The Fish going to pull me Overboard!!!" I would laugh and say, "Catch the fish bie/ boy, you can do it... It ain't/ is not going to pull you over/ off the dock..." I would just stand back and watch... He would fight this fish on the rod, and eventually pull the fish right up on the dock, all alone... I would be so proud of him, then I would mock/ tease him after he has the fish and say, "TUB, hold the chair, it going to pull me over!!! Lol" He would reply, "It felt like it was going to pull me over!!!" And we would both laugh at how scared he was... I would be so Proud of him, to see him actually catch Big Fish from his Wheelchair...

So ya, I'm up J.V.C. waiting for NI... And Matthew's brother Snoop calls my phone, and says, "TUB, I'm in Town, in the Park..." (that's where Snoop and sometimes Matthew hung out to when they were bored) "And this Guy just Slapped Matthew..." I reply, "Matthew is in a Wheelchair... What Shit you talking!!!??" He says, "Ya, this guy just slapped him and knocked his food out his hand, onto the ground... I was "MAD" Instantly!!! I said, "Well Handle it then!!! What's the problem??" (meaning teach that guy a lesson for fucking with Matthew) He says, "The guy kind of Big and Tall..." I replied, "What the FUCK!!!" I then said, "Ok..." (I already knew he was Pussy, well not Pussy but didn't really like to get into shit unless he had to, I guess... But this was a time to Activate/ act up, I thought!!!) I continue, "Well I'm up Warwick right now, waiting on Ni, when I get back Town, I'll come and Handle it!!!" He said, "Ok..." And we hung up...

I Can't Believe what I just heard!!! But I'll sort it out later For Sure... NI, finally comes, I link him (pick up) and head back city… I call my cousin Snoop, and he proceeds to tell me, "That he handled it, and it all Good now…" Ok, that worked for me… I make a note to go see Matthew and ask him all about it soon…

I had actually forgot about it though… Until one night me and my other cousin DANGELLO, are in a bar in town… The night is going cool, and we are getting ready to leave the bar, and My cousin, D says, "That's the Guy that Slapped Matthew right there!!!" And points to the guy… I look, and I know the guy a little… He is basically a No-Body that wanted a name in the streets and wanted to be Gangster… A guy that can't hang in the Hood because he not hard enough, but will hang in the City/ the park in town, and play Gangster…

The guy knew of me and had always basically kissed my ass/ super respected me, because of my Reputation… So, I say to D, disappointed, "Fuck man, I thought that guy was cool!!!" So, then I walk over to the guy, he was only about 5 feet away… I say to him, and not try to hide I'm irritated, "What's this, I hear of You, Slapping Matthew in the Park!!!" He starts to Plead innocence instantly… He said, "It wasn't like that, Me and Matthew used to Wrestle and Play fight back in the day…" I cut in and said, "But the Fucking Guy in a Wheelchair Now and you Slap Him!!!" He replied, "I didn't really Slap him, and Me and Matthew cool, we talked about it…" I say, "You know you Fucked up!!! And you know, if you touched Matthew, I'm Fucking You Up!!!" He replied, "I know TUB, but I didn't slap him…" I said, "Ok, but I'm going to ask Matthew, and if he says Different, it's going to be your Ass!!!" (He knew I was Serious, No, smiling and Joking Shit…) He said, "Ok…"

I go back over by D, and just so happen it was a girl there, that also hung in the park… I say to her, "Did that guy slap Matthew?? And Snoop handle it??" She said, "Snoop, didn't Do Nothing, and Yes he, Slapped Matthew…" That's all I needed to hear… I Immediately went and gave this guy one Punch with my right fist to the Face… Then Another quick one with my left… Now D, isn't one to fight, so I was surprised to see him, come over my shoulder, with an umbrella and was also hitting/ beating the guy in his head… The guy trying to run away now, but I ain't/ am not letting him get away… We were in a little back outside area of the bar and it had an alley to it, and he was trying to run that way, to get away from the licks/punches from me, and the umbrella beating from D, that he was getting…

My right hand has a hold of his shirt, so he can't get away… D, is still hitting him in his head, so he trying to duck from that… So, I swing my left and catch him good again… I swing again, and he was so scared he moved and I graze my knuckles on the wall… He finally got away after I got about 2 more good ones in his face… And then we just left the Bar, because most likely the police would be called, and I wasn't hanging around for that… The next time I saw the guy about a week later, he was saying Sorry to me… I told him, "Don't say Sorry to me, say Fucking Sorry to Matthew!!! And Don't Ever Touch Matthew again, because it will be Worst!!! But I have nothing against you (him)…"

My cousin D, later told me, he doesn't like to fight, but he gets Courage when he around me… I laughed… In my mind, I thought, Nigga you just soft… Plus he also knows, if I'm there, I'll keep him safe for sure… I remember I was with my First P.O. when this happened, because he had asked what happened to my knuckles, because they were grazed... I had told him, I was fixing my bike and my hand slipped... He believed the story... The first fight was for a good reason, I feel... Now the second fight was more for a stupid reason and because I was drunk I guess...

This night I was out swinging doors, a girl I had relation, (used to fuck) with in the past/ months ago, was having a party, but me and the girl wasn't really speaking... So as the night goes on, I decide to dance with her a little since it was her birthday day... I didn't try take it no further than that... But I had been drinking all night, shots of rum and all... At the end of the night, everyone from the party and people who chill out court street are just chilling around, because the clubs are closed now...

A guy that must have also had relation with the birthday girl in the past, starts to DISS / disrespect her out loud... Everyone laughing, including me, it was funny... He was saying how, she sucks his dick, and just clowning her... She must get angry and goes towards him... He instantly clocks this girl, in the face, with a right punch!!! The crowd goes, "Ohhh lol" He hit her good, and she was a solid/ thick chick, she buckled and almost went down... She regains her footing, and he clocks her again Good... He laughs at her, and then he still talking shit about her...

He had punched her So Good, it was Crazy... I didn't really like it, I thought he was a coward, he could have slapped her if anything... Them were some serious punches... Someone had walked the girl away up the street... He was still shouting shit loud up the street to her... She started to head back our way where the crowd was... Someone decided to shout out, "One on One", meaning him and the girl fight one on one… He says loudly, "Ya/ Yes, One on One!!!" I had seen enough…

As he still talking shit, I pick up one empty bottle and slip it in my back pocket… Then I pick up another empty bottle and slip it in my other pocket… I thought, "One on One huh?? I'm Smacking This Guy!!!" So, as she gets closer, someone says, One on One around the corner… They were talking about around the corner outside Social Club… I thought Perfect, no cameras around the corner, and it was cameras on the street where we were standing… He says, ya/yes around the corner, and they and the crowd head around the corner… I'm sure to walk close to the guy that's talking all the shit… I'm acting like I'm coming to watch the fight…

As soon as we turn the corner, I'm walking behind the guy and I take one bottle out, and Spank him cross his head… I think he turned around and threw a punch and it caught me a little… All I remember, I was standing over this guy just Punching and Kicking him, and saying with every hit, like when you discipline a child… I said, "How! Dare! You! Hit! A! Girl! Especially on her Birthday!!!" (I said it over and over, and was hitting him as I said each word) I was beating him, for hitting her on her birthday, and at the same time giving him a lecture… I was so caught up in hitting/ beating this guy once I started… I had his shirt pulled over his head a bit, and he was down and couldn't do nothing… Next thing I look down and his back is cut wide open… That brings me back to Reality… As I was beating him, the birthday girl went and got a bottle and broke it and slashed the guy across his back… All I saw, was Flesh and Blood!!! I stopped and then said to the girl, "Let's Go…" I took her to the hood to this chill spot I had and hit it/ had sex with her and went sleep…"

The next day, when I sobered up and I thought about the night before… I realized how Stupid I was, for Risking my Freedom, and Vowed to not get in Any More Fights while on Parole… It was too risky… And I know the guy had to get stitches across his back, for his cut… Good thing the guy didn't go to the police… I ended up meeting his baby mom later in life, we got cool… I only knew he was her baby dad, because she said, "That he told her, I beat him up out court street…" She said she didn't care, she was happy I did… I Didn't Care either…

Now the Last Incident… Around this time, my Baby was still young, and I had moved to the east side of the island… But I would still travel town daily to hustle, because now I had to pay rent… In an area of town, not my Hood, someone's Jewellery must have got stolen, and word must have gone around that I had received it… That weekend my BM (baby-mom) was away so I watched the baby… I picked her up on the Sunday and drove her home… I was heading back to the hood/ town area to get my hair braided…

When I get close to my destination, I get a call, it's my BM who I just left, not even 30 mins ago… She proceeds to say, sounding upset, some guys just Ran into Our House, and was going on All Bad, talking about some stolen jewellery, and they had a girl with them, and they made her slap my BM, as they threatened her… They also took her phone and some jewellery… I had Heard Enough!!! I knew I had just Left My House, and my Little Baby Was There!!! My Blood was on FIRE!!! I was Beyond MAD!!! I was ready to Kill!!!

This was a VIOLATION!!! A DISRESPECT So GREAT…
That Someone was Going to PAY!!!

I thought about Parole… And what would be the outcome,
if I get in Trouble… My Good thinking got kicked right out
my mind by the Anger… I said to myself, "I didn't give a
Fuck about JAIL!!! Someone was going to get Taught a
Lesson!!!" I was pissed at what my BM said, but that wasn't
what took me over the edge… I thought about how these
guys would actually, come into MY HOME, and my Little
Princess(Baby) is in the house… I was Super MAD!!!

So, the next thing I done was go to the Hood and get my
younger cousin SCOUT… I tell him go get our little nigga
JUICE… We all get in the car and I go speeding Home/
East, as I tell them what's going on… It didn't matter to
them, if I said let's Ride, its War Time, they Down period!!!
No questions, and me the same for them… I tell them
exactly what happened, and I told them my plan… My plan
was… My BM noticed/ recognized one of the guys and
knew where he lived(stayed)… So, I was going home check
on her, and then I'll get her to show us where the guy
stayed… We beat and kidnap him, so he can show us where
the main guy that lead the group that came into my house
stayed… The main one talking all the shit and made the girl
slap my BM… We beat the first guy, because he was the one
who showed them where I stay…

I made sure, No One Ever, knew where I stayed, so I'll
never be at home and get caught out… (niggas running in
my place) I had seen that too much in movies, and if I ever
got in that scenario, I'll be running in the house and being
the aggressor… So, I would take extra precaution… Also,

people in the hood start to think you rich when you got jewellery and bikes and a nice car… They think you got big money and/ or Big Drugs… So, motherfuckers want you to be slipping, just to check to see if you got it/ anything… If guys are scared to come to your house while you there, because they know you Wild, they will just wait, and break in your house when you leave… You couldn't win, so I made sure, no one could get to me…

Now this Ass, (one of the guys) knew my BM, don't ask me how he knew where she stayed… Hmmm, makes you think… So, he directed them to my address… So, Me and my 2 little niggas, SCOUT and JUICE, get to my house… I almost knock off my bumper to my car, because I hit the sidewalk ask I park, from racing… SCOUT says, "TUB don't mess up the car…" I say, "Fuck the car!!!" I'm Still Pissed Off/ Mad!!!

The neighbour watches the baby and we take my BM in the car, and she shows us where this nigga stays, I think they went school together or some bullshit… We leave her in the car, and we take the machete we had in the car and go to this niggas door… I knock on the door a few times, and no one answers… We break into this fucker's house, and proceed to search and take whatever we want… The guy stayed in the bottom apartment of a house… JUICE jumped in the window and opened the door for us…

When we got inside it was a studio apartment… The guy was known by my cousin Scout for selling big weed… We find big sandwich bags with small pieces of weed all over the house… We take them all and talk about how we caught him when he low on his weed… In the end we had about an ounce and a half to split… As I look around more, I see a machete on the bed, where it looked like he must have stopped back home after coming from my house and dropped it on the bed… It just looked out of place… I pick up the machete, and I pass it to Juice, and say, "We are taking it with us…" My attention went next to a Big safe in this guy's house… It seemed light, like it wasn't nothing in it, but I wanted to carry it to the car and open it later… Scout talked me out of it… I still feel I should have just took it… I had been waiting for an opportunity to hit or take a safe… We left it though, and we went back to the car and proceeded to drive towards town, where the other guy lived…

As we drove and talked… Scout let me know that he knew who the other/ main guy I wanted was, and where he lived… So, I'm going to the hood to leave my BM there, and grab my cousin to join us to go visit the guy… My BM let me know, that the guy knew I was on my way to him, because her sister went with one of the guys friends… And the guy was rounding up his boys, and they are waiting for me to arrive… I didn't care if he knew I was coming or not, he could have an Army Waiting!!! I was going to teach him a Lesson!!! How dare they come in MY HOUSE, that's DISRESPECT!!! Plus, my Baby was there!!! It was Definitely ON!!!

So, I drop my BM off and tell my cousin Snoop get in the car… I thought to myself, I know he won't fight, but an extra person will look good on my side… Push come- to shove, he probably would have helped if needed… And I also called my boy FAB… And he rode behind my car on his bike, as we headed out point area, to go get these niggas… As we get closer to the guys house, Scout is directing me on which way to go… We come to a narrow road, so we have to let a car through… It's a guy I went school with, I thought me and him were pretty tight, like brothers… He slows down by my window and speaks, I speak back… So, Scout says to him, "What's up with your boy, so and so, (says his name) going to TUB's House!!! His eyes widened and said, I'm going to turn around… I didn't think nothing of it, as soon as it was space I went through… I was on a mission!!!

I later saw that he turned around to be on the other guys side, and I thought we (me and him) was tight… I didn't fuck with him no more after that day… I was actually trying to fuck his baby-mom after that, but I could never catch her to talk… I would just see her in passing…

So now we go up the hill to this guy's house… I drive across his yard… He has over 20 guys in his yard, just standing around waiting for us… They saw my car when I drove cross slowly… I park about 50 yards away from the yard, but facing the yard way, and get out the car… I had a 2door car, so I pull my seat forward and say to Juice who was sitting behind me, "Pass me the machete and Don't let them see…" I didn't want the crowd to see the machete and get scared… He slips it to me and I slip it down the back of my jeans and put my shirt over the handle…

I look towards the crowd, and the main guy… Guess he thought he was the Boss and calling the shots… But he didn't know ME… It Was Already On!!! He screams out, "P.C.C.", to say let's go out P.C.C. which was a park area close, so we could handle this, or fight, or whatever he thought I came for… His Plan wasn't My Plans though… I thought to myself, "P.C.C., and this guy came in My House with his boys, and My Baby was there!!!" I immediately started marching (walking) towards the crowd at the thought of that… As soon as I start walking, JUICE follows with a baseball bat in hand… The rest where probably so shocked that we were just gone without a word said…

As soon as we got into the yard and close enough to people, JUICE starts to hit Every and Any-One in the Head with the base-ball bat… The crowd starts to scatter… My focus is on the main guy, and the closer I get to him, I slowly start to reach for the machete… He sees me starting to reach for something… He runs off a little and screams out towards the house, "Aunty call the police he got something!!!" Hearing this I go for him again/ rush towards him a little… He runs off a little and screams Police shit out again… During all the Medley/ Ruckus of people scattering from Juice still hitting people… I see the girl who went into my house… I knew her, we went primary school together, she was from a next Hood, up 42nd street… She was a known bad girl per say… I go to her and about to slap the shit out of her, her for slapping my BM, and coming in my house!!! She was a Hood chick and knew me and knew I didn't Play!!! As I'm about to slap her, she looks like she is bracing for the slap, and I think to myself, she better because I want to slap the shit out of her/ slap her hard… I'm hoping the slap will knock her ass out… I hear Scouts voice shout out, "Don't slap her…" So, I stopped last minute… She was clearly scared… And she was lucky SCOUT said it, because I was going to slap her up GOOD!!!

I next see the guy that showed them where I stay, he just jumped the little wall of the porch, trying to get away from Juice with the bat… By now Juice was on the Porch, banging people with the bat still… The guy that showed them were I stay was coming my way, so I grab him by the collar with my left hand, and think, I'm going to Punch him out!!! He was a lot taller than me and not a real slim guy… I was waiting to throw my punch, because I really wanted to catch him good and hurt him… He was scared and trying to get away, and get my hand off his collar…

He must have realized the size difference, and realized he was just as strong as me, so he decided to try and grab me… I saw the change of thought in his eyes, he went from being Scared to Brave… When I saw this, In My Mind, I said, "You think so Huh?? You want to get Brave!!! Take This!!!" So, at that moment, I Grabbed that Machete, the same one I had just took off his bed… I whipped it out from under my shirt, and I chopped him on his arm!!! The same arm he was trying to grab me with… He Instantly, screams out, in Cries, "He chopped me!!! He chopped me!!!" as he held his arm where I chopped him with his other hand… I instantly look towards the main guy I wanted, and I go for him… He Screams out now, "Aunty call the Police, he got a Machete!!!" I look back towards the street at my white convertible car and think, "I'm got to Leave!!! The Police might be here soon!!! And a Machete is an Automatic 3 years, and that would be, On-Top of what I Got Left on Parole!!!"

I Go For, the main guy Again anyway, I want to chop/ hurt him 2 before I go, but his Bitch Ass, won't stop running from me!!! So, I say, "JUICE, let's go…" Me and Juice, just walk back to my car, and we all get in and drive off… We are heading back to the Hood… In the car, they are talking about how JUICE was just beating everyone… I block them all out, and in my own world/ thoughts… I think about "It All" as I drive… And I think to myself, "I still want the Shit they took from my house!!! The Jewellery and Phone!!!" So, I go to the Hood, and park the car, put the machetes away, and then decide… I'm going back up there to the guy's house, "Right Now" on my bike, and get my shit!!! (goods that were taken) I decide to use the lock for my bike as my Weapon this time, in case they don't give up my shit, and if the police stop me, I won't get taken, because if they see the machete, I'm a Goner…

I ride back towards the guys yard, where I just chopped the guy… I'm alone on my bike and my Boy Fab is coming with me, riding his bike… I told him I'm going back up there to get my shit, and he said he is coming… I wasn't worried, I would have gone alone… When I get back to the yard, there is No One at all there… It was totally quiet, no people, cars, or bikes… I then decided to go back to my BM, and make her call the guy number… I called this guy and say, "I want the Gold and Cell phone you took from my house NOW!!!" He says, "You just Chopped Me!!!" I cut him off and said, "I Don't Give A Fuck!!! I will come down your Job and Kill You!!!" The goons were making a name for themselves in the street, so I also said, "I'll send the Goons, down your job to kill you…" I told him, "Don't play with ME!!! You guys came in My House and My Baby was there!!!" He said, "I can't get the Gold and phone, someone else took it…" So, I said, "Fuck That!!! You Showed them where I Stay!!! You Better Pay Me Then!!! I want 2grand, $2,000 dollars, and if Not, I'm coming for you, because you Disrespected ME!!!

He agreed he would pay in 2 weeks… He didn't have a choice really!!! He was also trying to say something about my

BM... I said, "Fuck all that... Just Fucking Pay ME!!!" I told him he was to give it to my BM's sister to deliver it... I never spoke to him again personally, but 2 weeks later, my money was Delivered... I left it as that, and Me and Him issues, were no more... Luckily, he didn't go to the Police, I would have been back in jail for sure... His name did come up again soon after, this was even before I got paid in the 2 weeks... One day I'm in the Hood chilling up LOGY's house and my close nigga KEN came to me all angry, talking bout I shouldn't have done it... (chopped the guy) I could go back jail, and talking some BM shit... I replied, because he was my close boy, like a brother to me, and I knew he could fight... We guys had been beating guys up together since school days... So, I said to him, "I don't give a Fuck about Him!!! (the guy I chopped) Those Guys came in My House when my BABY was there!!! And you defend him, because he sells you big weed?? Fuck you 2, if you going to defend him!!!" So, he was like, "O, you want to Fight Me Huh??!!!" I said, "It's What-Ever Nigga, but Don't think you going to get a Fair One!!!"

I knew his Energy Level, I would have to Dig him/ knife him, or we would have to fight all day... Because we both had Super Heart and we both was Tough... He heard my "Warning" though, and knew I wasn't playing... He just said some other shit and then rode off the hill and went home... He came back later, and said he just didn't want to see me back in Jail, because we were like Brothers... We did used to screw girls together, and all that bullshit, growing up... And he said, "The first time I went jail for Murder, that hurt him, so he didn't want to see me in trouble again..." I understood, because I remember when the Judge said, "Sorry Mr Darrell, I must give You, LIFE in Prison..." I instantly heard Ken in the back of the court make off angrily at what the Judge Bitch had said… So, I understood him, but showed him, its PRINCIPAL when it comes to MY BABY…

The other time, the guy I chopped name came up was about 6 months later…Now I was actually wearing a gold chain, that I Knew was stolen from the guy I chopped, but I didn't care… I had brought it from someone, but that's what the word was… So, my cousin Shorty(CAVUN) says, "Your boy, you chopped… called me and said, you are wearing his chain…" I told my cousin, tell him, "He Paid me to Leave him alone, so just keep my Name out his Mouth!!!" After the closeness, of the whole situation of me getting in trouble, I had to MAKE SURE, from this point ON, there is to be no more fights or Nothing!!! So that guy's name never came back up… But his friend, the main guy that Lead the Group to my house, name did… I was waiting to see this Nigga!!! I hadn't taught him a lesson Yet, but I wasn't worried, when the Time was Right, I'll see him, and it will be Instantly ON!!!

In the guy's world, (that led the group to my house) His mind must have been on me, because every time I would see one of my boys, because I'm cool with everyone… They would say, so and so, asked about you, wanted me team up with him against you… And they would all say, they said to him, "Why?? Why you bother him for??!!! You supposed to leave that ONE Alone!!!" Everyone already knew I'm cool, but don't Fuck with Me… I can get Dangerous…

A next time Scout called me and said, the Goons, mainly FINGAS of Park Side, wanted my number… We were always cool, but not on the number level, so that's why Scout called me first to see... I said, it's cool, give it to him... FINGAS(R.I.P.) calls my phone and says he wants to meet me in the Hood... I say, "You sure?? What's it all about?" Alarm bells are going off in my mind, I don't know if the Goons can be trusted... I'm seen them guys be cool with each other one second and they Waring/ fighting, each other the next... FINGAS says, "It's all Legit..." So, I went and met him...

I got to our meeting spot early... We decided to meet by Scouts house down Bottom Road in the Hood M-TOWN (Middletown) in an hour... When I park my car, I pull out the machete, and place it close to where I'm standing... Just in case... FINGAS comes and gets out that Big Jeep he used to drive, and he cool, I didn't sense no bad vibe... He said, "That nigga you got Beef with, said you broke in his place and took his chain... He trying to get it back, and said he will pay me if I get it back for him..." FINGAS then said, "He will give me a cut of the money..." Someone had broken into his place and took his shit, but I showed FINGAS, I didn't know nothing about it... I told FINGAS, "If I go into his/ that guy's place, I'm waiting for him to get home!!! I'm not just going to steal shit and go... I want that guy BAD!!!" FINGAS felt were I was coming from... So, FINGAS and I, gave each other Respect, and he left...

The Chain I had on, was the guy I had chopped chain from long before... The guy that led the group into my house, was the one who's house recently got broken into... Scout said later, that he saw me stash the machete, before the meeting, and was wondering the reason... I said, "I'm got to be safe, I didn't know what he wanted, and you know how them guys Get Down…" He agreed…

…CHAPTER 7…
…FIREMAN…

I ALMOST Became a FIREMAN… I was looking all over for a job, checking the newspapers every day and checking online… I see the add in the Royal Gazette News Paper, that they are recruiting Fireman, and anyone between 19 or 45, (I think) that was healthy and wanted a Good career, or some shit, should apply it said… I had always said from young, if I couldn't get a job when I become a Grownup, I'll be a Fireman… At my young age, and at that time in my young mind, I thought it was Easy just like that… But now I'm Grown, it won't be as Easy as I thought, because now, I had a Criminal Past, and was still on Parole… That's what I thought anyway…

I kept seeing the Fireman add in the newspaper daily, and since I was filling out Applications for Every type of job, and sending My Resume to whoever would look at it/ all jobs that were Hiring… I thought, "Let me give it a try, and Apply for the Fire Service… I didn't have Nothing to Lose, and Maybe I'll get Lucky!!!" So, I applied or sent in my application to see if I got a response…

About a Week later, I don't remember if I got a letter, e-mail or call… But my point is, I got Response/ a Reply from the Fire Service… They said its about 6 to 8 parts, (can't remember exact) To the whole Process, but you/ I, have an interview for Stage One… This was GREAT News, because on the Application form, I "Had" to mention my Conviction, and I also mentioned I was still on Parole… So, they already knew that I had a Troubled Past, and they were Still Interested in Interviewing Me… I thought to myself, "You got a Start!!! Let's see, if you can pull it off, and Really, Become a Fireman…"

When I got my response/ reply, they gave me the Date of my first interview… I was Proud I made it to Stage One… So, I showed the Progress I had made, and also shared the info, with my P.O… I think I still had Mr. M, as my P.O. at this time… He was Super Proud of me, he was in shock, that they would give me a chance… Not that I was bad, but since I had a criminal past… My P.O. didn't know that on my Application… I Stressed the Fact, that I was a Changed Man, who just needed a Chance… I pointed out how I was a Christian now, and all that criminal past stuff happened when I was young, and now I was a Different person… Going through it all, and Jail had changed me for the better… I told them, I was, A Born-Again Christian now, and lots of other stuff, like Everyone Deserves a 2ND Chance… So, all in all, since I got a Response/ Reply… I guess that shows that people/ Bosses at any type job, are "WILLING" to give people a Chance, that LEAVE their Criminal Life Behind and are Truly on a New Path of Life…

Yes, I was a Born-Again Christian… I also believe in the Rastafarian Religion… So I must big up, "Emperor Ras Tafari Makonnen Woldemikael HAILE SELASSIE 1st of Ethiopia… But like I said, I definitely am a Believer in Christ and God… But I was more a Personal Relationship type of person, not all the church shit… But for these people I was using the Church Angle... I guess they liked where I was coming from... I thought, it sounded all good on paper, but let's see how the Interview Goes...

So, it's time for the Interview... I had to go to an Office Building, down the end of Front Street somewhere for the interview... I made sure I was shaved up looking all clean, and had my hair done... I had on a white button up shirt, and some money green dress pants on, and a matching tie with a nice design/ flowers on it... My mom had got the clothes for me from somewhere, probably one of them thrift shops, but either way I was looking fresh, and I was all clean... I was ready for the interview!!!

When I think about it, Mr M. was actually my P.O. at this time, and I think this all happened when I went off the road... It all became clearer because I remember, the Cute girl, that I had as my rider, right after I had the Portuguese girl as my driver... This cutie was working at a hotel at one time before I met her, and she found a Man's size, white gold, man's wedding ban, with a nice size diamond on it... So, one day she gave it to me... I had kept it for the diamond, I didn't like white gold, it looked too much like silver to me, so I never wore it... I later in life used that same diamond from the ring, and put it in the Crown Pendant I got the jeweller make...

So, to top my Professional look off... I pulled the wedding ban out my secret stash at my mom's house, and decided I'll wear the males wedding ban, and I'll tell the people in the interview that I'm Engaged... They were sure to ask about the ring... I get to the interview... In this interview I'm sitting across from 3 Older males... One of them have on a uniform, like he could be Head of the Fire Department… They were all basically in control/ Head of the Fire/ Hire Department… So, the interview begins… When I walked in, I was all polite and shit like usual… Good afternoon, to each and make sure I shook their hands… I shook with a nice firm grip, but no to over-power the person hand I was shaking… I wanted them to Connect to me, not feel like I was trying to hurt them… That's what I was thinking anyway… Then I sat down, and thought, "Here we Go… I wanted this interview to go PERFECT!!!"

They were all nice Polite gentlemen… First, they asked about my conviction… I knew that be first, so I was ready to talk about it… I Down-Played that shit to a T… I made it seem like, I was just helping the lady the night of the stabbing… And how I almost Died, and God kept me alive for a reason… And I pointed out my young age at the time, and how my Lawyers Sold me out… They Agreed/ Understood… Technically, I wasn't lying… I went on to tell them, how I got a Life Sentence and Appealed and it all got Reduced, when I should have been Freed, for the 2nd time… And I done 5years inside and now was on parole… And I only had such and such time left on Parole, however long I had left and, how "It's All Going Good…"

I had told them the whole story, and then I went on to tell them, "How I found GOD inside jail, (which I really did) and how it all changed My Life… Now, I'm a Devoted Christian, and I go Church Every Sunday… I also Volunteer, at the Church and at Church Functions…" One of them was a Church man, so he asked what church I attend… I just picked whatever church came to mind and said it… He knew the Pastor, of the church I said… Thank God, he didn't ask for the Pastor's name... I went on to tell them about my Baby Girl and how I am Engaged... They acknowledged the ring and was surprised because I was still young, and taking the step of marriage... I probably told them I met her in church, I can't remember... But I do remember I told them that my soon to be wife, asked Me to Marry Her... And I said YES!!! And we had planned to set a date soon, but we might just do it next year some time, to see how things go...

They must have been thinking, this guy Life sounds like it is going Great... Then they started all the talking, and got into all the Fire Job shit... Like all the stuff, that the job Entitles... They told me they get like 200 applications, and only 40 will start the process... And out the 40 in the end only 8 to 10 will really make it... So, they will review, and finish their interviews, and if I hear from them, then I made it to the next step... I thanked them for their time, and I was gone... I leave the interview and think to myself it went ok... I would just have to wait and see...

A month later, I get a call... I was selected for part/ interview 2... I was Super Happy... The Hard Part was out the way... They knew about my Past and was Still Willing to give me a chance... I just had to pass all their test now... It was a few tests they said you had to pass, a fitness, Psychology test, and also basic fire stuff tests... It was a lot of steps they said, but I was just taking them One Step at a time, and do my best and hoped I passed...

The 2nd part/ stage of the interview/ test, all the chosen 40 or so had to meet at the Fire Station, for Introduction... They split us in groups of 10 and took us to do 4 different tests... They monitored us, and took notes... They made us climb all the super tall ladders and shit, and had us crawling through smoked out tunnels to see if we can find our way through different drills... After these drills they let us go and I guess you had to wait for your invite to say you Passed to the Next Stage...

I guess Luck was on My Side, because I had made it to the next stage/ 3rd stage!!! I started to take it All Serious now, and said, "Maybe I was Meant to be a FIREMAN..." This 3rd stage I knew I would pass... It was a Fitness test... We all had to meet up Nationals Sports Center, which is actually The Bermuda's National Stadium... I was thinking I must be able to pass a fitness test... The test was much harder than I thought in the end, and I realized I wasn't as fit as I thought... But it was all timed, everyone's personal time was noted for everything... I just pushed myself and done my best... After that day, Yes, I was Called Back Again for the Next Stage!!! I was Beginning to get Excited, and think I can Make It...

During one of the stages, one of the Fireman, that was taking us through a drill, pointed out to me...That I might have to Cut My Hair/ braids to be a Fireman... I protested a little instantly, so he also said that Women had long hair in the Fire Service... It was just required to be kept up some way, while at work... But most times, the Guys just cut their hair... This was the only thing I had to really Debate... Did I really want to cut my hair?? I Loved/ LOVE my Hair... I didn't know if I could cut it, but anyway it Wasn't an issue right now... So, I'll worry about that later, if I become chosen for the Job I thought...

So, I went through a few more stages and I was basically in… I was "Sure I'll get the Job as a Fireman!!!" Now I swear I was down to the last 3 stages, this where it was getting interesting, because I'll be hired if I pass the last 3 stages… It was a Psychology Test… What they done was, let us take a long psychological test… That was actually the stage… But they then take your test and evaluate it, and the psychologist also reviews it, to see if you mentally stable to handle the horrors of the job… Shit like being first to an accident and finding a dead body, what would you do?? How would you react?? Or if someone leg cut off from an accident… Or if it a family member, you find crashed up, what would you do?? Crazy shit/ questions like that… But I think they were just testing your thoughts, and then at the final stage when you sit with the actual psychologist… They want to see can you give the same answers or be in the same frame of thought, when you took the test the first time… Because they knew people always try to answer the test questions with the answers they think the people want to hear… It was all Mind Tricks I thought… And then I thought, "I made it this Far, I'm Got This!!!

So, after that stage it was, the Final 2 stages… First, you had to go to their Doctor to get a Full Medical, to make sure you were healthy enough for the Job, and a hair sample, drug test… And the Final stage was sit down with the Psychologist guy… And I got called and scheduled for the medical, so I knew I passed the test I just done… And the Medical Test would be cool… I thought I was Healthy… And as far as the hair, drug test, I definitely wasn't worrying about that!!! I had only smoked Weed ever in my Life, and I hadn't smoked for years now… At least 2 years… Plus I was getting Drug tested by my P.O. every 2 weeks anyway… So, I Knew I was cool…

Before I went to the 2nd Last stage of becoming a Fire-Man… Which was a medical and hair sample, I'm debating if I should go get my hair done… But then I think, nah don't do that, because they going to have to cut a piece of your hair anyway… My hair was already in Braids, so it be better for them to take out an old braid and cut it, instead a fresh done braid… I don't worry about getting my hair done, and I just go to the medical meeting…

I go to their (Fire Departments) medical doctor, like I was scheduled to… His office was up at the Police Headquarters up Prospect… He gives me a full medical and takes my blood and shit… And then he picks a braid and tells me take it out, then he cuts a piece of hair from the root, and he wraps it up in foil and says that's enough hair for the sample… Ok that was fine with me… He said he does the test and if everything ok, he sends the results to the Fire Department… And They (the Fire Department) Will Contact Me and schedule your/ My Last Interview… I walk out the Doctors office, and think, "TUB, you Made It!!! I just have to Get Through the Last/ Final Stage!!! And I will Be a Real-Life FIREMAN!!!

A week went by, and I was Waiting for the call from the Fire Service People, to tell me when my last interview would be… They DIDN'T Call… Instead I, got a Call Back from the Medical Doctor!!! I saw the Number, and knew it wasn't good… I also knew it was him calling, because I swear I had the doctors number saved from when I first made my appointment… The phone said Fire Doctor, that's how I saved the number and knew it was him calling… My Mind

PANICED!!! I thought to Myself, "Why the Fuck is the Doctor calling you back for??!!! He said he will only call if something is WRONG!!!"

I Instantly thought the WORST of the WORST!!! I wondered if something I had Done, in the Past had caught up with Me!!! I thought about All the girls I had sex with in the Past with No Condom!!! I started to Feel Sick... I wanted to Throw Up!!! I said, "TUB, What the Fuck is Going On??!!! He Tested You, could it be AIDS!!!" Tears came to my Eyes!!! I thought to myself, "Catch Yourself, you Don't Know what he wants!!!" Then I thought, "Fuck that!!! TUB, change your number and don't look back!!! Fuck being a Fireman!!! If the doctor is Calling You, then something is Wrong!!! Do you really want to know?? Can you Live with some Crazy Shit Like That?? NO!!! So, Change Your Number!!!"

When I didn't answer the call... The Fire Service Medical Doctor had left a message to say call him, he wants to See Me... That message drove me even more crazy!!! The more I thought about the Doctor Calling, the more Scared I got... My Mind was Playing Tricks on Me, Big Time... And my Crazy Thoughts didn't help... I decided to say, "Fuck it, I'll give the doctor a call, and go see him!!!" I call him, and I schedule a time to go see him... When I called, I was ready to go see him... So, he can just tell me what the Deal is... And whatever he tells me, I'll just have to Deal with It!!! He told me I can come right up and visit him, when I called...

I was so Fucking Scared going up to this Doctor again!!! I prayed to God on my way... I was still thinking the worst of the worst... I thought what Life would be like, to live with

Aids... I was sick, and tears came to my eyes, at the thought... I wished I never Ever fucked any girl without a condom... I hadn't had much sex without a condom, but I didn't know what else to think... I then thought, "I wished I was a Virgin!!!" My life was Over, I thought... So, I get to the Doctors office, and take a deep breath and enter his office... It seemed like as soon as I got there, he was ready to see me... I thought, "That ain't/ isn't Fucking Good..." And I wanted to cry, but I shook it off...

So, I walk into the Examine area and sit down... I instantly say to the Doctor, before he can say Anything!!! I say, "Doctor Just Tell Me What it is??!!! I can Deal with It!!! Aids?? Any other Disease?? Just tell Me... Please??"

He looks at me in Surprise, at my Question... He then grabs his notes and says, "No, Mr Darrell... All your Test came back clear of Anything... No Aids or nothing... BUT, Your HAIR SAMPLE... Came back with "Traces of Cocaine..." So, you are Out of the Application Process for the Fire Service Job... Sorry..."

I was So Relieved, to hear them words!!! I thought, "No Aids, NOTHING!!! Thank GOD!!!" But I didn't know if I should be Happy, he said I'm Good and not got Nothing wrong with me... Or, should I be SAD, he said I'm Out from my chances/ steps of being a Fireman!!!

I instantly say, "COCAINE??!!! That's Impossible!!! I'm NEVER done Cocaine in my Life!!! There has got to be a Mistake!!!" He said, "Sorry it's No Mistake, that's what the Test said..." I said, "That can't be!!! You got to test it again or something?? I have never used any drugs before period, just weed... Plus I'm on Parole and get drug tested every 2 weeks!!!" I was trying to say anything, so he could test my hair again... Because I was in Shock, at the Reading of Cocaine!!! He said, it's too late, the test took you Out of the Process Already... The only thing I can Suggest, is you APPLY again, next time they are looking for Fireman Recruits... I thought, ain't/ isn't that some Bullshit... But what was done was done... So, I thanked him, and left...

He probably wondered why I was thanking him... I was thanking him for not telling me nothing crazy... lol... When I walked away from the building, I thought about how I was feeling before I walked inside the doctor's office, and I laughed and thought to myself, "TUB, you're a Softy, you were all scared and ready to cry for nothing, lol... You Knew it wasn't nothing wrong with you, plus you just had a baby..." I thought, "Yes my Mind was Fucking with ME" I then told myself 2 things... "CONTROL YOUR MIND and EMOTIONS NIGGA!!!" "And You WON'T BE Fucking/ Having Sex with no one With-Out a Condom Ever again!!!" That Shit was too Scary for Me!!!

I was Still Puzzled about the whole Cocaine reading, though... I was telling my P.O. how I was making out in the Process of becoming a fireman... I couldn't tell him the reason, I had failed!!! I just said, I just didn't get a call back... I still couldn't figure out the reason, for that out-come of the test... I thought, "Maybe, they decided they didn't want a guy on Parole as a Fireman... And it was all a Conspiracy to just kick me out, because they didn't think I'll make it to the End, and here I was, so they had to put an end to it..." It could have bin that, because Cocaine seemed so far-fetched to me!!!

I knew I hadn't used Drugs/ that shit, Ever in Life… And then it Dawned on me… Like a light bulb, being turned on… I was still hustling Crack (cocaine rock) at night in the Hood sometimes… So, maybe from me being in contact with it/ touching it at times to sell it… I then must have touched my hair, and that left traces of it in my hair… I thought, what the fuck TUB, you should have got your hair washed and done like I was thinking before my medical/ hair test… I Fucked up Big time!!! I had all the Bases Covered, to make sure I got the Fireman Job, and then I Miss one major key factor… From that point on, in the back of my mind, I blamed Hustling/ selling drugs/ crack, for me Not Getting the Dream job of a Fireman!!! I guess in the End I wasn't meant to be a Fireman… I didn't want to cut my hair anyway, so I guess it worked itself out… But one thing, all this did show me, even though I Fucked up and didn't get the Job… That even though I'm on Parole and had a troubled past, if you (I) apply yourself and try, you never know, people will probably give you a chance… Sky's the Limit…

...CHAPTER 8...
...GETTING TO THE FINISH LINE...
V.I.P. LIVING/ DREAM BOAT

During All, that been going on in My Life, I have managed to keep my P.O. Happy and stay out of Jail, and also not do anything Else, that might get my Parole taken away from me... I have been out of Jail on Parole for like 6 years now... I was still hustling a little crack on the side, and also weed if the price was right... But all in all, the Street Money, had slowed down severely... The young goons where so bad, that they were robing the drug dealers and even robbing the crack heads/ people that do drugs... So, no one wanted to sell anything to Town guys anymore... I didn't have to worry about this because I had links all over the island... But since the people that smoke crack refused to even come to the area, the market was Dry... They (the young goons) were shitting on their own doorstep... And as a result, everyone was suffering, even them...

It was No Loyalty!!! They were also stealing and or snatching niggas/ each-others and other people's chains, like crazy... Well not just them, it was happening all over the island, but it was happening much, much, more in town areas... Everyone started to not wear their Gold in fear that they would get robbed... No one was Exempt!!! They were even fighting each-other and robbing each-other's drugs... I saw all this and knew they/ No One was to be trusted... I had sold my old chain and had brought a next link chain from this guy… Later in life I then got a Big Gold Pendant made when I was working at one of my many jobs, and money was real-good… The pendant design came from, a broach my mom used to wear when she went out to dinner… It was in the shape of a Crown… I always wanted a chain and Pendant that No One Else, had or had ever wore it before… So, I got the shape of the crown, made in Pure Gold… It was a Beauty/ It Is A Beauty, I should say… The jeweller at the store Link to Link, down Flatts, made it for me… They have since closed down the store or moved somewhere else… I always had a chain once money started getting good, they would come and go in the streets/ Hood… Guys would trade or sell them to each other also… But now I had MINE and it was here to Stay!!!

I continued to wear my chain, even though it was so much stealing from each-other going on… I just stayed On Guard and Never was slipping… I wasn't hiding either, if someone had balls enough, then I say go for it/ come for it, if you want it that bad… I just hoped the person was prepared for what they will start… No one really tested me for my chain… Plus I was back in the gym and starting to look all muscular again… As Parole is concerned, I feel I'm done Good, since I'm managed to stay out of Jail for 6 years, and I'm got 2 years to go on Parole… Damn, I'm just so tired of these Peoples Rules!!!

Around this time, things got Extra Bad in the Hood!!! Before it was, sort of, A Town against Country/ West, War… Basically the young guys from each of these areas, didn't like and wanted to kill/ fight the guys from the other areas… It all Puzzled me, because not only are most of these guys related someway, close Relatives and distant... But because mostly all the older guys, around My age and up, didn't really have no problems with each other... Unless it was a personal Beef... It was never, Beefing with a stranger because you know he lives in a certain area!!! So, I wondered where the HATE, for each other came from??

First it was a, Town against Country thing... But then the younger guys in town, started Waring, with each other... So, now Town, had a Full Fledge War started/ going on... It was Middle Town and Park Side against 42nd... This was SAD, for me to See, because both sides were literally shooting and killing each other... So all I saw, was My Friends Killing my Friends, both ways... Middletown was always My Hood, and those Park Side Youths/ Goons were cool, and them 42 Guys had been my Boys Forever... (from young) And it seemed like just a few years ago when I first came out of jail, I was playing football with guys from all them areas... They were playing football together for Boulevard Blazers, Dandy Town, Devonshire Cougars, and other teams... And now a few years later they are shooting each other... I'm thinking WOW, they all used to PRAY together at the end of football training... And now look at how they Treat Each Other!!!

The older 42nd guys my age was also getting caught up in the war... It was nothing I could do though... I was just Lucky I was Not in ANY WAR... I could go West, and did very often, and I wasn't in the Town thing and didn't even know what none of the Wars were really about... But as long as No-One bothers, or threatens me, it's nothing to do with me... (the wars) I just thought it was all Stupid and Sad!!!

My WAR was with the System!!! I had to Finish Parole and get theses Fuckers Out My World!!! And stay out of trouble in the meantime… One day I was sitting on my mom's Porch… She had moved back to the Hood, close but not exactly in Middle Town… I was sitting on the Porch one evening just chilling, and my Little Nigga BIG B, comes by to just check on me… BIG B was a straight Gangster, All the Way… He rolled with the young goons, and didn't play… He liked the Wars… And he would rob a guy quick, he used to carry a chain with a bike lock on it… He used to like to use it on people… I'm seen him Split some one's head wide open in the hood, because the nigga said the wrong shit to SCOUT… He used to always come check me… Me and him got tight through my little cousin SCOUT… Now, BIG B was like my little brother, we would go check girls together also… Even though we didn't see each other every day… ME, SCOUT, BIG B, JUICE, and my other little nigga JU-JU, were all like, "Brothers!!!"

So, this day/ evening, BIG B comes check me, at My Mom's spot… He was one of the small few, that actually knew where to find me… When he comes, I just so happen to be, sitting on the front porch chilling… He comes hails me up, and asks me if I'm good and all that… I say, "I'm good just here, going to make a run soon/ go somewhere in a bit…" He then says to me, "Guess what I'm got??" I said, "What you got??" He then Pulls out a Gun… It was a silver, and black 9mm Glock, I think… I said to him, "Your Crazy!!! Let me see it…" He hands me the gun and replies, "TUB, you know the War is ON!!!" He paused, then said, "It's only got 3 Shots, (Bullets) in it… It had 5 bullets, but I let off 2, over the wall down Boat-Club at them 42nd guys… He paused again, then said, "I'm got 3 left for them though!!!" I said, "Fuck YO… The War is that deep??!!!" He said, "YES, Fuck them guys!!! They would try get Me, so I'm going to get them!!!" I just shook my head…

The GUN, is much Heavier then it looked… I said to him, "This shit is Heavy…" And then I aimed it towards the yard and acted like I was aiming to shoot something… Then pulled it back in, looked it over quickly, and then started to wipe the handle off, and any part I touched, so my finger prints wasn't on it… He was watching me, and laughed at me and said, "You ain't/ do not have to worry about all that… I Clean it, Every Night…" I laughed and said, "I'm just making sure…" I had finished wiping it off anyway, and passed it back to him, with the sleeve of my shirt… After that he said he is going up the Hood for a little while… I guess he meant directly in Middle Town, where everyone sat off down Bottom Road… I told him be safe, and shout me in a bit… We exchanged pounds (fists) and he was gone…

When he left, I thought, "My little nigga is Hard… I hadn't Held a Gun since I was in the Army… And when I shot the 9mm in the army it didn't seem that Heavy, but that was a long time ago…" And then I thought, "This nigga carrying a GUN like it Legal!!!" I guess these are the times… Those youths/ guys really had a war going on… I wondered again, "What are they all Waring For??" The next thought was, "They are falling into the "SYSTEM'S TRAP!!!" Black men Killing each other for Nothing!!!" We can't get No Justice under this SYSTEM and In This SOCIETY, as it is… So, that's even More Reason, we should stay out of Crime and Jail!!! Then I thought… "DAMN, The War is Real!!!" My next thought was, "Damn my little nigga Crazy, but At Least I know where to get one (a GUN) if I ever Needed It…"

Then I thought, "Fuck all that crazy shit!!! Do you want to go back jail??!!!" "!!! Stay Focused!!!"

I can finally see the FINISH LINE, but with my LIFE STYLE... I Wonder if I'll Make It?? Since money was slow in the Hood, and Everybody and Anybody was getting Robbed, or Caught by the police... It made me stop and Think!!! I said it's, "No way everybody is just getting in trouble with the law, like that... I was surprised/ stunned... All the people I would check for shit was caught in something... Everybody was going jail or had a case... The shit was Island Wide, everybody was getting in trouble... I said, "Fuck this Shit, the only thing I could do with that hustling lifestyle was be lazy, and not make no one's time to work... It wasn't profitable..."

It Wasn't really worth it/ hustling... Because the money wasn't there no more, I was basically Suffering, everyday..." I also thought back to that time when I almost became a Fireman, and I knew, if I Wasn't for Hustling, I would have Got the JOB!!! So, I somewhat still Blamed the hustling for me not getting a Great Job... I thought it's Time for a Change!!! Plus, Parole almost Done... And, I definitely don't need no Court/ Jail, Bull shit now!!! So, I decided it was finally time to, "Give Up Hustling" for Good/ All Together, and look for a Real Job again... Plus with 2 years left on Parole, I didn't want to Chance, getting Caught Out or doing wrong/ breaking the Law No more... So, that's when my Hustling Career Ended!!! JOB searching here I come!!! So, from there my Quest for a Real -Job Started...

So, I go on Many Interviews once again, and No Luck... I start to think, maybe I should try and go back to hustling... But I decide, No, give it a little more time, something is got to come up... It must!!! Risking my Freedom Every Day, can't be the answer... So, I decide to keep looking and going on interviews... Someone is bound to feel me, I'm a good/ cool guy and I can be a good worker, if I can just straighten up and make my time to work... I'll definitely have to Party less and make my time when I do get a job...

It seemed as I won't get a Job, nothing would work... Then one day I happen to be listening to Ms THANG on the radio... I used to listen to her on the radio, while I was on the inside of jail/ Prison also... She doesn't know it... But her on the radio, helped me and I know for sure, much others, get through their time inside... She was a God-Send/ Sent from God, to keep us entertained so we didn't go Crazy, while locked in that damn Box/ Prison... So, this day on the radio, she is being all Inspirational... And then she plays, that wicked song that I like... It was the Big BERMUDIAN Artist "SLANGER..." The song had the lyrics saying, "Stay Focused and Be Conscious" I thought, "SLANGER is Right!!! If I Stay Focused, a Job will have to come!!! I'm got a Job before... I just have to stay Focused and keep Pushing!!!" I thought about how I knew SLANGER Personally... I remembered one day, (in jail) a few guys and I was playing court football on the jail basket-ball court... I swear my boy REBEL from down Crawl, was also playing football with me and the few guys this day... We wanted to play 4 on 4, but we had 7 guys... This was during recreation... So, SLANGER looked like he was probably going to take a run around the field... I knew he could play football and was good, so I said, "SLANGER come play ball with we guys??" He was like, "Nah not today..." So, all the guys started saying, "Come on SLANGER, come play??" He was still like, "Nah I'm good..." No, he didn't play court

football with us that day, but I thought to myself,
"SLANGER is a Focused Guy…" I think if it was me, I
probably would have just played… He must have been
thinking, "Playing football is you guys plan today, not
mine…" I admired how focused he was… And years later,
we both are free from the clutches of Jail… And now he is
doing it Big, making music, doing shows, even doing songs
with Big Jamaican Artist… Me and SLANGER had always
been cool since we had met… He has a Lot of BUD/ Good
songs, and this song was one of my favourites…. So, as I
listened to the song, I said Yes, that's what I'll do, "Stay
Focused and Be Conscious… And A Job Will Come!!!"

I kept sending out Resumes… Then I land a job as an
Apprentice Baker/ Pastry Chef… Finally, a job with decent
Pay… At the interview, I Hadn't told the one English Guy/
Boss, that I met/ had the interview with, about me being in
trouble in the past… I think I just left that part blank on the
application, and since he didn't ask, I didn't say… The other
interviews I did tell them I had been in trouble in the past,
and I didn't get the job… So, when I didn't tell them, this
time I got the job… I was to start the new job in a few days,
the next Monday…

Before I start the job on Monday… The guy/ new boss calls
me, because he found out about my conviction, and he asks
why I didn't mention it, in the interview… I just said it
slipped my mind or some shit… He says he will call the Big
Boss and call me back… He calls back about an hour later,
and tells me I still got the job… He said, "Luckily, He liked
my energy, so he vouched for me…" So, I still had the Job,
and I was still Starting on Monday…

The job was fine, an easy profession to be honest… I was learning all about Baking Bread, and making Cakes, and Cupcakes and Decorating them and all… I had to learn All the Bakery and Pastry shit basically… Before you knew it, I had it all down, and they loved me… All nice people, they were just too passionate about the job… I didn't mind that They Love what they do, but don't be Mad that I don't Love It… It was all just Work to me… And I hated making peoples time… The Money/ Pay, was Good so I couldn't complain too much though…

My P.O. thought it was great that I got this job, so this kept him off my back… The Next Big Thing, that happened in My Life was, I saw a speed boat/ Jet boat that I must have… I linked with the owner, and he said he will sell me the boat for 17thousand dollars… ($17,000) This was a Steep Price, because I didn't have Money like that, and I had stopped hustling… But the boat was so wicked, and it had the new Bermuda Money sprayed/ designed across it… 100's 50's 20's all new notes in the design… I Wanted it, and I worked my ass off, so I could get this boat…

My quest for the boat was hard… I had Bills and shit also, but the Bakery pay was ok… I just had to Stay Focused…I would always get up to about 7grand saved, and then something would come up… Like my car had to be fixed or some shit, and I had got my own apartment around this time also...

To push myself, and make myself get the Boat… I called the owner of the boat and made sure it was still available… He said it was… I told him I'm Sure I Want It, and we Set a

Date when I would come buy the boat… I think it was in 2 months from now, but the Date was Set…

Towards the end of the 2 months, I finally reached the 17g by doing a lot of Overtime, and other little job hustles… Like cutting grass with one of my boys when I was off from work, and I borrowed the rest… I would start at 6am and finish at 3pm, so I had a lot of day left to do different jobs, I wanted that Boat so bad!!!

The date comes that we set up, that I would Finally Purchase the Fresh looking, Boat… I call the guy, and at first, he won't answer… On the 4th time… When he does answer, he goes on to say, he sold it to someone else, for 21 grand… I was Mad as Fucks, we had spoken a week ago to re-confirm!!! I wanted to Beat this fucking Guy, for wasting my Time!!! I used to speak to the guy in passing when I saw him, now I fucking hated him… I said, "If you wanted More MONEY, you should have just said that Last week, when we spoke!!!" Now I had all this Fucking Money and No Fucking Boat!!! I wanted the BOAT not the Damn Money!!!

I guess Everything Happens for a Reason… Because soon after, since I was so disappointed… I was thinking of just buying a Jet Ski and saving some of the money… But a close friend of mine, saw I was So Disappointed and wanted me to be Happy… So, they went online, and saw a boat, that they think I might really like, and they wanted to show it to me… So, the day I saw the boat, My Close friend came pick me up to take me for a drive… We were going for a drive to see this boat she had seen On-line… The Boat was up Dockyard at Spar-Yard Boat Lot/ Garage…

On the way up to see this boat... During the Drive, I'm telling my close friend I want her to take me a Hotel Tonight... We had stayed at mostly All the Hotels in Bermuda... She would just pick ones, so we could stay, just to see how their rooms were, and for just something different to do... I LOVED staying in the Hotels... Growing up in the Hood, I wasn't used to all this Luxury Living all the time... Soon after time, I was so used to it, I had mostly stayed in all the hotels and also guest houses...

Hamilton Princess was one... Southampton Princess was a regular... I liked to stay in the rooms up on one of the high floors, 4th or 5th, so I can have a nice view... Elbow Beach Hotel was also a regular, the rooms down by the Beach were nice/ A favourite of mine... Elbow Beach rooms up in the hotel were ok too, but I preferred the rooms on the beachside... Grotto Bay Hotel, was also a regular, when I think about it... There were also places like, Bright-Side, Pomander Guesthouse, Clear-View, COCO Reef and even Cambridge Beaches Hotel... Just to name a few more... (It was a lot more places though) I would also be able to order room service, or drink whatever I wanted out the hotel fridge/ mini bar... And in Bermuda that fridge/ mini bar shit, is always extra expensive... With this close friend, we also went to Dinner at like it seemed every restaurant in Bermuda... She got me in the Bad habit I have, of like going out to dinner... So soon we would only go when I requested, and was in the mood... And today as we drive I'm telling her I want to go Hotel...

She says, "Well this is what we can do... We go see this boat, and if you don't like it, we can go to whatever Hotel you want and stay the night... But if you, do like the Boat, you give me the 16 grand you still got left and I'll put the rest, and you get your Boat, and you Pay me back later... Shit, that sounded like a Great Plan to me... I thought, "Let's go see this Boat, and then I'm going to a Hotel to Chill..."

So, we drive up to Spar-Yard and park... It's boats all around, but nothing I would really want... I follow her around the corner, to the water side were more boats were... I see a few boats that catch my eye, then she stops by one with a cover, and when I take a good look at it... I knew Instantly, it was the one for Me!!! It was, MY DREAM BOAT!!! This was like the one I wanted before, but definitely an UP-GRADE!!! The boat I wanted before didn't have a box in it, it had to be fixed... But this one had a working box and speakers with a I-pod connection... That other one had one engine... This one had 2 engines, so it would be much faster, and it was just as Beautiful... I fell in Love with it... This one (jet-boat) was 23 thousand... ($23,000) I had spent a grand, so I had 16 grand left... So, I said to her, "This Boat is Mine!!! I Love it and want it now!!!" She said, "So, No Hotel??" I said, "No Way, lol... I want this Fucking Boat!!!" It was/ Is PERFECT!!! I had to go back to doing Overtime.... I got as much as I could, and borrowed the rest, I wanted this boat now... I gave my "Sweet" close friend, the money I had Raised, which was basically the 23grand... I didn't want no one say they helped me in the end, that's why I didn't just give her the 16 grand and let her put the rest in... The money I did borrow, the people didn't know what I was borrowing it for... Everyone knew they would get paid soon... I just said it an Emergency... So, I dropped my close friend, the money/ cash and told them, "I want them to do, what they got to do, to seal/ close the deal... I just want to Own the Boat!!!" So basically, I left everything else, up to them to sort out... A week later, she/ my close special friend, then tells me she wants to have dinner at the Restaurant "BOUCHEE" on front street... I had never been there before, so I agreed... I had a feeling the dinner was to tell me about my boat... When we sit down to dinner, and she finally hands me the KEY to MY NEW BEAUTIFUL DREAM BOAT!!! I didn't show it, but I wanted to Scream and jump up and down like a kid!!! I wanted to Kiss and Hug her!!! I was so happy inside!!! "My Beautiful Boat, WAS ALL MINE!!!" O, Life was Sweet!!!

The only time I really felt Free was when I was on My Boat out in the Ocean... I swear it was/ is the Prettiest boat in Bermuda, everyone loved/ loves it... White Rich People, would come boating by on the Ocean, and say, "We like your Boat!!!" One time I was out with a, bunch of girls, and this Police officer guy, shouts out to me... He was always cool... He was on a, nice big speed boat/ pleasure boat, with a wicked blue strip, and he had some sexy girls with him 2... He says, "How you like my Old Boat??" Shit... I replied, "Thank You Very Much!!!" I super Loved My Boat... I was happy he sold the Boat and I brought it and it was now My Baby... (smiley face) Also, If I took a girl out on that boat, guaranteed by the end of the trip, I had fucked/ had my way with her... Even if that wasn't my plan, it would just happen... Even if she said, I'll go for a ride, but nothing is going to happen, we just friends... I would say, "Ok cool, let's go..." The boat was Magic, trust me!!! Enough days I would call in sick to work, and go Boating... Also, during this time, someone new, I had just kind of met, and was just getting to know... Ended up Pregnant... So, I would Soon be adding a Baby to my Little Family, that consisted of only Me and My One Daughter I had now…

My daughter didn't mind an Edition to our little family… So, in October, we welcomed another Little Princess (Baby Girl) in our little family… Yes, I was still close with My Awesome Mom and great Sisters and everyone else… But theses 2 little ones were MINE, and I would Always Protect Them!!!

I remember the day the baby was born, not only because I was waiting for MY 2ND, New Princess… But also, because I was happy, I could leave work, and not have to come back for a few days… I was ready for Parole to End, so I could X everyone, who told me what to do, out My Life…

I was thinking, the first thing I'll do is, tell my P.O. kiss my ass and have a good life, and don't call me no more, and I would Quit this job for sure… I wanted to Start Over, FREE!!! Because, I looked at Life, like I had never been Free… Believe it or not, I used to drink worst then I do now/ before I went jail… So, I have always been trapped by the Alcohol/ my environment, but I realized this downfall when I was in jail… And ever since then, I'm wanted to be Free Completely… And in 2 years, My Life, will Start, when Parole Ends and I Quit Work … O, I can't wait for that Day…

Life is looking good, got 2 sweet baby daughters, working steady, got my Lovely Boat, and my Awesome convertible car, O and, can't forget My Big Gold Chain!!! (smiley face) You think I would have kept my nose clean, (stay out of trouble) but no a month later, I'm with my mom drinking… So, we decide to take a drive to the east side of the island to get more drinks, its Friday night and its around her

Birthday… We go St. Geo, to visit a Bar, but I know I'm got to be work the next morning early at 6am… We get east and go Mini Yacht Club, my mom's boy/ mate, Thomas, is behind the bar/ bartender… He got the drinks flowing… (coming to us) Plus I had bin fucking with this Sexy, Sexy, girl down that side… She was also at the bar… We were all playing pool and drinking…

I look at the time, it's getting late… I tell my mom I'm going back town, because I got work in the morning… She said she is staying at the bar… I say cool, well I'm heading out… The girl I'm seeing down East, doesn't want me to leave, because I usually stay longer, if not all night… But I can't be late for work, I'm almost on my Last Chance because of my time keeping… So, I left and started driving home/ town… I decided to take the quiet route town, so I won't see no police…

It's a nice Night, with clear skies and lots of stars in the sky… I'm had the roof of the car down all day and it is still down, so the breeze feels good… I guess the breeze made me start to feel all the alcohol I had drank, because I started to drift to sleep… I was fighting it… I drifted off again and woke just as I was about to touch the wall, with my car… At the last second, I swerved away from the wall… I was the only car on these back roads… I thought just get home, you can make it… Next thing I know, I drifted off again, this time I woke when my car touched the wall slightly… I said to myself, "I better just pull over before I fuck up my car, or even Kill myself…"

I pull over in the next Bus stop… (In Bermuda you can park/stop in Bus stops) It was the Harrington Sound School bus stop… I wish I could stop the story, and say that was it, I rested and went home… But Nope, I won't be so lucky tonight… The next thing I know, I hear someone say, "Hello are you alright??" I Opened my Motherfucking Eyes, and the fucking Police are standing at the Door of my car!!!

My Stupid Ass, must have pulled into the bus stop… And Went Straight to Sleep!!! I didn't turn my car lights off, I didn't put my convertible top of the car up… I didn't even turn the Fucking Car Engine Off!!! Nothing!!! All I could do was reply to the police officer and say, "I'm alright…"

He said, "Ok, because I thought you had a seizure or something… You were just out, and all the lights on, and car started…" Then the Million-Dollar question came!!! "Have you been Drinking tonight?? Step out the car…" I put the top up and turned off the car… I knew where this was going, he already had the handcuffs in his hands… I thought, WHY ME!!! (SAD FACE) They took and processed me and all that bullshit, and here I was, Back in a Cell!!! My World seemed like it was All Over!!! Shit, my second baby was probably just 2 months old, and I'm in this Bullshit again… I just tried to go sleep, as usual when they put me in a cell… When I sobered up a little, I was super Devastated/ Up-set!!! I tried get them let me out/ go, so I can make work in time by 6am, but they didn't want to hear it…

I thought to myself, "I should have just stayed down east…" I knew this was going to End Bad, and this was just the Beginning!!! I would be taken off road again, and fined heavy!!! I will Definitely, have to see the Parole Board Again, and who knows what they going to say… This the second time/ D.U.I!!! And then I'll hear it from my Boss at work... AHHH, It's no End!!!

They Finally let me go, from that Damn Police station, with my paper to say when I would have to go before the judge for the charge for D.U.I. (Driving Under the influence of Alcohol) I called my Boss, he already knew, because my mom had called him when she found out... My P.O. had been switched, I had a chick now, at least I won't have to deal with the old P.O... I called her and told her what happened... Next, I got a lift back to my car... It was in the same spot... That damn Bus stop... And to think, it was a parking lot right next to the bus stop, that I could have went in and parked and been cool... Well it was done now, so I'll have to deal with it...

Getting the D.U.I. up-set me Bigtime... That fine ass girl I had down the east, didn't have no sympathy for me... She just said, "See you should have stayed East..." I'm thinking, damn that bitch is cold hearted... She didn't even care, I feel my world is ending, because I got the D.U.I... but so it go... Her man was in jail, so I guess I was just filling in, until he got out... She was a beauty and great company, so I didn't mind... I was happy that we were cool because I had always, Adored/ wanted/ was attracted to her... With me off the road again/ no trans, we drifted apart anyhow...

I felt like, I had let Myself down... I was so close to the end of Parole and here I go and slip/ fuck up... I meet with my P.O. and she tells me, I'll be going in front of the Parole Board, and the date I'm to see them... Since she had seemed cool, all this time before when we met, I decided to speak openly... I said, "Yes, I Fucked Up Big Time!!! But the

Parole Board can't send me back Jail…" I paused, thought, then continued, "I don't mean, they Can't because I know they Definitely Can… But I'm got like a year and a half left, I'm been good for the last 6 ½ years, somewhat… I'm working steady, and Plus I just had another Baby and got another young daughter… So, they would have to be Heartless to Revoke my Parole, and send me back Jail…" I guess I was trying to make myself feel better, and thinking Positive…

I left the meeting and went on with my day… I went court soon after and got another year off the road and fined… Good thing my last D.U.I. was like 4 years ago, because I would have been off the road for double the time, for getting caught again so soon… I was still Very Sad at being taken off the road, I felt like I had Failed!!! This time off the road was Much Harder than last time also… I didn't have someone steady around me to take me everywhere… I would get through this though…

With no transportation and being bored, I was hanging more out point area at the horse stables, out the creek… Next thing I knew, I had a Pet Horse called Smiley… He was a Beautiful Big Horse… And my big daughter loved him… So, this became my new past time… And when it got warmer, I still had my boat, I didn't need a license for that… You never really got stopped on the water anyway… Especially if you weren't breaking none of the water/ boating rules…

I decided to Pay the $300 and do the Driving awareness course once again, that would let me stay off the road for 9 months instead of the 12 months again… Since I was still off the road, my life was basically, getting a lift to work, my daughters of course, feeding and taking care of my pet horse Smiley, going to the gym and Boating... I still had that meeting with the Parole board though... That was coming soon... I knew that Won't be a good day...

GERNEL L. DARRELL

...CHAPTER 9...

...MEETING/ CLOSE CALL....

The wait for the Parole meeting, was mind boggling... I wondered what the outcome will be... My 2nd D.U.I., the Parole board won't be happy... I was super nervous, but in my mind, like I told the new woman P.O., that they, (the Parole Board) shouldn't send me back jail because I had done good so far... I was 6 plus years in to an 8year Parole Order... I had just had my 2nd baby-girl bout 3 or so months ago... I hadn't been in trouble, while on Parole, except a next D.U.I. and that was over 4 years ago... I was working steady at a local supermarket, in their Bakery section... And they only got good reports from them... My Boss also had to write a letter to tell the parole board about my work, and I had a feeling he won't exactly point out my lateness at times, was causing an issue... Plus after the D.U.I. night, I made an extra effort to get to work on time, even though I had to find a lift, or ride a pedal bike to work...

The Day of me meeting the Parole Board, finally came... This time the meeting was held in the New Court Building, that was built on court street... It was around the block from the old court house, but this one, also had the new police station, and court services, and the Probation dept., all in the same building... I think I was at work before I walked to the meeting... I wore my company Logo uniform and stripped Baker pants, hoping that this will help my cause... They couldn't send a working man to jail, for a mistake... Could they?? Not if they are fighting for a better island/ Better Bermuda, because the young black male, had a hard time finding decent work... And if the young black male wasn't working he was being part of the problem, not the solution...

Before the meeting, I met with my P.O... I ask her, "If she thinks everything be Ok, for me?? She reassures me, it should all be ok... It was one other guy to see the parole board also... He was one of the little niggas that hung out the street... He didn't look to happy... He went in to his meeting to see the parole board first... I sat outside in the corridor, while 2 Prison officers stood guard... I paid them no mind, because I was still free, so they had no authority over me, Yet...

They were making small talk amongst each-other... The other guy meeting was finally over... The 2 officers that came out the meeting with the guy, said immediately to the other officers, "He is going back up top..." I was like W.T.F(What the Fuck), this was exactly like the same scenario of the time when I saw the Parole Board the first time... They didn't just grab him and take him away like they had done to the guy about 4 years ago... This one protested, and they just try to talk him down, and tell him he must go with them... Then they discussed quickly which 2 officers would take him to the awaiting van, that was going directly to Westgate/ Jail... He didn't have a choice really... Guess they didn't just grab this one, because he was much more well known then the last, and they knew they would have problems the whole time with him, once it got started...

But that was his fate… Mine was still to be seen… I said a prayer… I said, "God, Please, don't let these people send me back Jail, You Know I Can't handle It!!! Please get me through this!!!" Before I went in, to see the Parole Board, my P.O. went in before me… I guess it was procedure, so the P.O. can give the Parole Board their part, and answer any questions before they saw you… Because most times you saw them the Parole board, your P.O. is the one, that tells them of your issues, or if they don't agree, that you are following your rules, so your P.O. makes you see them… So, my P.O. comes back out, and it was my time now, to go into the meeting…

The 2 officers escort me into the meeting… I walk in… I'm in my frail, soft mode now… I say good Afternoon to Everyone… Got to be polite and ass kissing, but not too much… (I think anyway…) Now this time, it's about 8 people again… The main guy speaking, is or was an X politician, Ashfield Devent… He was basically from back of town… I knew he was overall a cool guy, so I thought to myself, maybe they won't send me back jail… Plus he had to know my mom, I hoped…

As soon as I sat down… He said sternly… "This matter we have here is a Second D.U.I., this is Very Bad!!! What do you have to say??" I started Pleading… I say, "I know this is Very Bad, I PRAY, that you people don't send me back Jail!!! I have No excuses, it was very stupid of me, I have just had a second baby girl, she only 4 months old, and my other daughter just 4… Since I just had another baby, and it was my Mother's birthday, she convinced me to have 2 drinks in celebration… And I don't know if the alcohol had an effect with my Work Out Supplements, but it made me feel weird, so I pulled over my car... I wasn't even driving at the time... But I didn't take the Key out the ignition, so I'm Guilty..." I paused, and then continued... "And the first D.U.I., I didn't know I was unable to drink... All I do now, is spend time with my 2 daughters and my Pet Horse..."

One of the other guys on the Board says, "You have a Horse?? What type?? I ride horses also..." I say, "It's one of the Big Bud-wiser type horses, a Clydesdale... My daughter loves it..." I could see on his face, he was pleased, with my answer... A next man on the Board spoke up, I guess he wasn't liking all the friendliness... He said, "Ok that is all good... But what is this we hear!!! That You, TOLD, your P.O., We Will NOT Lock You Up, or better word, "CAN'T" Send You Back jail, or Revoke Your Parole, because you just had a BABY??"

I couldn't believe my Fucking Ears!!! I thought quickly to myself, "How, could she do this!!! (sad face) These people will send me back jail just because they think I'm Cocky/ arrogant... The thought of them sending me back jail, because they heard, from my P.O., I said they CAN'T send me back Jail!!! That Broke my Heart Instantly!!! As a man, we or I, would fight my tears in front of people, but not today... The thought made tears come to my eyes, I wiped them away and started talking... But I wasn't wiping to stop them, just brush them off my cheeks... I hoped I looked Pitiful and Sad, so they could see what their Actions would do, if they thought about sending me back jail...

Yes, I was also acting a bit, but that shit was 90% Real... After my quick thoughts and one of them handing me a napkin... No one really wants to see a grown man cry... I Replied, "It wasn't even like that... All I said, to her, my

P.O. was, that I'm bin on Parole for 6 years now, and I'm stayed out of trouble, and I'm also working as a Baker/ Pastry Chef at Super-mart on Front-street... And I also just had another baby girl... So, they, The Parole Board would have to be Heartless, to send me back Jail because I'm been trying Really Hard, and I know You People, have the Power to send me back... I would Never act if you Can't!!! And I don't want my Babies visit me in jail... I wiped my eyes with the napkin...

I think I had done enough tears, to make me look innocent/ sincere and merciful... Another guy asked me, "Do you think you have a problem with Alcohol, and need counselling??" I said, "No, I think it was the mixture of Alcohol and workout stuff for energy..." And I'm also taking, the Driver Awareness Course, and to pass that you have to go to their classes and also go to 3 "AA meetings" as part of the course..." They then told me to wait outside while they decide/ come to a decision...

As I sit outside and wait, all I'm thinking, "This Bitch, (my P.O.) trying to get me in trouble... I just told her what I thought at the time, I wasn't trying to say it like I was Untouchable..." I wondered if my little show in there was enough... They called me back in, like 15 mins later... The 2 officers escorted me back inside... I sat down and wondered what they will say... I look around the room at their faces and think, "Here we go... What will happen??...

The Ashfield Devent guy spoke up again, and said, "They were satisfied it was a mistake, and told me I have to do whatever class or counselling my P.O. suggest about the Alcohol situation... They also told me to Leave the Alcohol

Alone!!! And do not come back in front of them, (The Parole Board) again because, next time they won't be so Nice!!!

I Thanked them for not sending me back Jail (my exact words) and said I won't be back in front of them... They got me sign and told me, I could leave... The Prison officers walked me back out the room... Before I left the room, the guy who said he rides horses said, "Take care of the horse..." I reply, "I will..." Then I walked out that room and had a Sigh of Relief!!! That was such a Close Call, it wasn't funny... I thought to myself, "I must stop putting myself through crazy shit... Today I was lucky, Thank GOD!!!"

...CHAPTER 10...

...REDEMPTION...

...ULTIMATE FREEDOM....

I'm Glad that meeting shit was over with... That was a Close Call!!! Now I could put it all behind me... I thought about my P.O., I wasn't mad that she had told the Parole Board that crap... I just knew I couldn't speak openly with her ever again... I thought, since I'm still here at the building, I might as well see when she, (my P.O.) wants to meet with me next... I went to the P.O. section desk and asked for her... It was a security guard that they also had by the door to pat you down and check your pockets to make sure you had no weapons, even though the clerk was behind a glass desk and buzzer door... She said my P.O. said she was busy, and she will call me... I didn't mind... I guess she, (My P.O.) thought I was upset at her for telling the Parole Board damaging stuff... But No, I was just glad I was Walking Free... Now I only had to make my work on time, and stay out of trouble... I only had about a year and half to go, I must make it to the Finish Line!!!

Life was pretty much routine, the basics, work and little ones... Being off the road I couldn't just roam how I liked to, in my free time... And it was winter, so the Boat was in storage... I ended up spending more and more time with the horse… I was learning all about the horse and I guess the horse was learning about me at the same time… We were like Besties… I found Peace in just walking him at first because I was new to horses… And it's always someone around to be a mentor… And a little older guy that I became real close with, like brothers… His name was Chicken… Or that's what he is called… He was just Awesome, he could make the horses do what-ever he said…. He became my mentor… (when it came to horses) He wasn't just awesome because of the horses, this fucker could also Ride a motor cycle/Scramble, Drive a car like a race car driver, and Race and fix Speed Boats… He was into everything and could do it all, above average level… Shit that took a lot of skill to do, he could do easily…

I still had my Jet Boat, and Chicken had multiple boats, so once the weather got warm… All the Boat Parties started… So, I went from being scared of horses to spending mostly all my time with the horse… Then warmer weather came, and the boat goes overboard for use… That's when I linked with my other Boy Darion… Me, Big D, and Chicken were a team… I had finally come back on the road… I was happy about this, summer was here, and I would make the best of it… I had let my car sit up too long and it had problems, and the garage said it be too costly to fix… So, I decided to get rid of it and send it to the car graveyard and not sell it for parts…

So, I just had to ride my motor bike for now… The bike I had brought was from one of my X friends… It was a new brand, but the colour was a darkish purple/ pink, black and white… Most guys would have changed the colour, but I liked the colour, only because I noticed the police didn't really stop me/ look at me as a threat, because it looked like I was just riding my girl-friends bike… And the less they bothered me the better, especially since I still had time left on parole… I still had my expensive life style, so I also had to do overtime and little work hustles to make money… I wasn't playing with hustling in the streets no more, it was all too Risky… I had a year left on Parole and had a few close calls, in the past, so I had to retire/ give up selling crack or weed or breaking the law in any way… My goal was to just finish Parole and start Life Over…

I had to Work Hard, I wanted another car… I missed having the option to drive… And now I was on the Road, it was only Right that I treat myself to a car… I heard of a nice car for 8grand… So, I went see it… My boy Gary from my Hood was selling it… It was a Beauty, and I wanted it… After some time, I finally got enough money and I get/ buy a MG, 2seater convertible for $8,000… It was second hand, but it was Awesome!!! It had nice rims on it already and a nice box with TV screen inside… I soon found out MG's are fast, but not good for Bermuda roads, because the speed limit so slow (35km) and you can't open up the car to the speeds it needs to go all the time, so you start to have issues… I had to change engines in the car and sold it as soon as it was fixed…

I wasn't happy that the MG didn't work out, and cost me a fortune to fix… I probably lost (spent more out then needed) in the end, as far as finances… But I was determined to get another car, but something better this time… I was hanging hard with my boy, Big D, and he had a Mercedes, a nice new model too… So, I also had to get something nice… But I was into convertibles, and more so, white ones… As time went by, I was still working hard, and trying to save for a car… And then like it was sent from Heaven!!! A white Drop Top, BMW popped up… My older boy OATS linked me with the seller of the car… It was actually my boy Ni, from J.V.C. daddy who was selling the car… Ni's daddy/ the owner wanted 16grand… It was going to be Mine for sure!!!

It was a Classy Car, and this one also had a TV screen, and expensive box inside… I finally brought the car… I was rolling BIG now… I would drive to the dock or beach in My White BMW Convertible, music Blasting… Park, and then walk right into the water to my boat, or to the dock to my tied up Pretty Boat… Start the boat, and the boat music system would kick in and Loud Music would start playing… I was looking like KING of the EARTH for Sure!!!

Everyone thought I was RICH, plus I also had on my Big Gold chain, but I just liked nice things… Everything was going Good, I'm still Partying, but I'm not Drinking and Driving, no more… That was a start… Definitely, didn't want to see, no damn parole board for that shit again… I can see the End of Parole soon, got just under a Year to go… I think of my favourite Reggae artist, BUJU BANTON… And of his song DESTINY… Then I think, "I Want to Rule My Destiny!!!" I can't wait to I'm Done with Parole!!!

Now since I'm partying, I'm not making it to work on time, so that's becoming an issue… I think I got down to my last chance… The Boss was going to fire me, if I was late again… And I was thinking about as soon as Parole ends, I'm going to Quit… Not because I don't like the job… Because I wanted to start my Free Life, FREE… No Boss to

tell me nothing/ answer to, and no P.O. to tell me nothing!!!
I would Finally be in Control 100%... Because in Jail I
realized that growing up, I got caught up in my family's way
of drinking, and their way was breeding Alcoholics, and not
even conscious of it... So, I vowed to drink less, (while
inside jail) if I ever got out... Now I was out, and still getting
caught in the trap of Alcohol... I'll have to Fight the
demons harder...

Believe it or not, I was drinking less now, then I was/did
before I went jail, but never the less I was still partying and
getting caught up in the moment and over-drinking... And
nights of partying, I always drank too much, once started... I
thought to Myself, "Is the issue for me the drinking, or is it
trying to drive when I drink??" Because other than the
D.U.I.'s, I wasn't getting in much trouble with parole
because of the alcohol... But then again, the drinking was
bringing issues at work, because of time making... But I
didn't want to be working there Anyway!!! So, either way if
I'm got to make 6am, to work mornings, I'm going to be
late, because I really don't want to be there... I also thought,
"I must Stop the Buck with me!!! Can't have my daughters
drinking and partying like me..."

I decided to Quit the job, I was done with the Place, and
decided to Quit before they Fire me... Parole wasn't done,
but I could just tell my P.O. I'm off from work, on the days
I saw her... And this worked... She would ask about work
and I'll say, "It fine, off today... I'm just got to keep making
my early time..." I would always wonder before I went to
the meetings, if Today would be the day, she tells me she
knows I quit... But she never had a clue... She would say, "I
was at your Job, and didn't see you..." I'll say, "I was

working upstairs that day…" Once the meetings started and she asks about work, I was relieved because if she asked about work, she didn't know I quit… And my luck got better, she had a baby, so I got a new P.O… And since I was almost done with Parole all together, (smiley face) She (my new P.O.) didn't think I wasn't working…

I quit the job sometime in January… A few months had passed, and things were going smooth… My P.O. wasn't bugging me really… Then one Regular day, I had taken a ride on my bike, to the east end of the island… My cousin Ian, went with me also, but he rode his bike as we went down… We decided to stop a second down St. Georges Cut Road… We had parked the bikes and were standing by the sea water, Ian having a beer and a cigarette, and I'm having a soda or drink… I get a call from my P.O… I see the number and I'm Alarmed, I think maybe she has found out, that I quit my job and didn't tell her… I answer the phone… The first thing she ask is, "Are you working today??" I could hear in her voice I wasn't in any trouble… So, I say, "Actually I'm off, why??" She says, "I need to see you, it's Urgent, can you come in now??" I said, "I could be to you in 2 hours…" She said, "ok, that's fine…" I wondered what she wanted, but I wasn't worried… Not working was the only Parole rule I was breaking…

I rode back town and went to my P.O.'s office… I sit down to the table for the meeting, and I ask her, "What's up??" She has papers in front her… She said, "Since you asked about what Day exactly, you finish Parole…" (I think I had a month or 2 left and wanted to be sure…) She continued, "We looked at your Dates, and We Must Apologise!!! You Were Finished Parole, back in January, and it was now like

May… I couldn't believe my Ears!!! I said, "Are you Serious??" She said, "Yes, I'm Serious!!!" And showed me the Original Form with my dates… She said, "She told me to come in, so I could sign my papers, and that be the End of my Parole… So, I'M DONE!!!"

I was Super Happy!!! I signed my Papers, and told her Thanks and Left… I walked out the office, and to the elevator, smiling the whole time… I couldn't Believe it!!! I had Finally Completed my 8 Years of Parole!!! I was So Full of JOY… I walked out that Court/ Court Services Offices Building, and Instantly, I Felt FREE!!! I thought to myself, "I won't have to come to this Building No More!!! I won't have to Answer to NO-ONE!!! No Boss, No P.O., No Parole Board, No Court… I was Finally, in Control Now!!!

 That trouble I had got into, one drunk night years ago, was finally All Over!!! Finally, I was Completely Free!!! IM THE BOSS NOW… From the beginning I was waiting for something to come and save me from sin/ evil… I Thought Honesty would be my deliver, and just make it all go away… But no, I had to Wake- Up and realise, it's a Cold World… And all along, I had to Save MYSELF, and give myself My REDEMPTION!!! I am My Own Super-Hero!!! I'm FREE, to follow my dreams, whatever they may be… I'll have to think on it, I thought… Decide what I really want to do with my life… It felt like a Big weight was lifted off my shoulders… Like I was stuck in a Night- Mare and now I'm finally Awake, and it's Finally All Over!!! THANK GOD!!!

I walk to my Bike and reflect… Now I can Live My Life, and Travel… Then I think… I'M FREE, I'M FREE, I'M FREE!!! I Didn't know how I would reach This Day… But now this Day is Here!!! And I have my Health, Sanity, and Peace of MIND!!!

I think of the Whole Thing… My up- bringing, Me being Bad sometimes, Me Drinking, Me Slapping the Guy, Him stabbing Me in the chest and puncturing my right lung, and then Me Stabbing him back in his chest and Nicking his heart… Me wanting to Kill him, and then Me starting to Die myself, but making it Hospital just in time…

Then finding out I had a punctured lung and blood was going into my lungs… Then Him being found Dead the next day… That could have been my last day/ night, on earth also/ the end for me… Then the whole Nightmare of court with the Life Sentence and Jail… That Prison cell with 23hours a day lockdown and one hour out… All the Years Behind Bars… Then ALL these Years on Parole!!! Yes, I was Very Bitter Inside!!! And I guess I still am, for the "System" locking me up, because I felt I didn't deserve that outcome!!! Especially since I was honest…

But I guess God kept me alive for a reason and Made me go through the Whole Ordeal to Help Me See the Light… And make me Realise, The Life I was Living, was leading to No Where/ Destruction or Even Death!!! And he had to give me the SHOCK and BATTLE OF MY LIFE, To WAKE ME UP!!! So, I guess it was all worth it… But what a Price to Pay for a LESSON… (learn from me) It was a Very HARD Road, but I Fought On… And I Refused TO LOSE, And as A Result… *I WIN!!!*

!!! VICTORY/ FREEDOM IS MINE!!!

...The End...

GERNEL L. DARRELL

Conclusion....

In Book 1... Travel with me through my Life, of Hard-Knocks... From a young toddler, growing up in the Hood, and all my Adventures... And at the tender age of 21, I was working and looking towards a better future... Until one day, in the Blink of an Eye, My Life Changed... All my hopes and dreams were Crushed, starting by me going to JAIL/ PRISON for the First Time, so I don't know what to expect... I was Charged with MURDER... And had to await a Trial for my Freedom, that was 6 months later... 6 months later when I was Sure I'll go home, I totally fuck up and Blow Trial, in a Self-Defence case I thought... And walk out of Court with the Worst Sentence Ever!!! LIFE IN PRISON!!!

In Book 2... I take you through my Whole Time inside this unknown place called JAIL/ PRISON... I deal with the Pressure of a Life Sentence and knowing I have No Chance of getting out of HELL/ JAIL, until at least 15 years pass... This was the Hardest Time in my Life... I became Real Cold, and had to Delete all Emotions, so I don't go Crazy... A Year later, I Appealed my Conviction in hopes of Being Freed or a Retrial... It didn't work out how I hoped, but it got a little better, and I walk out the Appeals court, with my time reduced from a LIFE Sentence, to a 12year sentence... And my Murder Charge Reduced to Man-Slaughter... I meet a lot of Crazy People, during my Time in Jail, and have many ADVENTURES... I do 5 years exactly to the day I walked in Jail... And In the end, I convinced the jail/ court "SYSTEM" to Release ME on Parole for 8 years...

Book 3 (This Book) ... 8 years of PAROLE is No Joke... Trouble Chases Me... I CONQUER ALL OBSTACLES, AND MY PAROLE IS DONE!!! and I'm FINALLY FREE!!!

As I look back on my 3part True Life Story... I see how LUCKY and BLESSED, I am to have got through it all!!!

I give all my Praises to GOD, He guided me through the Belly of the Beast/ and help me learn the Lessons, I needed to Learn...

I feel in Life, Everything Happens for a Reason... So, if I Love Myself Today, then I have to At Least Respect my Past... That's why I decided to not sugar coat My Story... And give it to you Raw and Real!!! And with all I'm been through, I still believe, Life is What You Make It!!! And no matter what circumstances you go though, In the End, The Choice is Yours, how you deal with it... It all starts with the MIND...

My story is different from All others, because from the beginning, it was a battle for me... I was a product of my environment and then I felt I was Wrongfully Jailed, so I Refused to CONFORM to the SYSTEM!!! ANY PART OF IT... And the War was, Me Against the System!!! So, Victory/ FREEDOM was my ONLY GOAL...

Like I said in Book 1... My LIFE, is truly like a movie and some may Love MY STORY, some may hate it and the choices I made... I am not condoning any choice I made or anything I done, and I don't know if I'll do it the same again... I'm just telling the story how it happened... But in the end, Life is about Learning... And one thing I Learnt,

144

No Crime Pays!!! And JAIL Is a place for NO-ONE, Especially ME!!!

But in the End...

> ...I DID IT ALL...

> > ... MY WAY...

...REDEMPTION... (The Action of Saving or Being Saved, from Sin, Error, or Evil)

... I FOUND MY REDEMPTION IN MY WRITING...

Thanks for Reading...

About the author…

GERNEL L. DARRELL, was Born in Bermuda on December 11, 1978…

Attended… Prospect Primary School, and Warwick Secondary School…

Gernel is the Author of…

REDEMPTION… A Real-Life SAGA, BOOK 1…

(Book 1… Worked on in London, England, UK)

REDEMPTION… BOOK 2, The SAGA Continues…

REDEMPTION… BOOK 3, The SEQUEL, to My REAL-LIFE SAGA…

(Book 2 and 3…Both worked on in Bermuda)

Check out my You tube videos…
https://youtu.be/mQGHCEHW0ZU

Also check out my Author Page at Author Central…
https://www.amazon.com/author/gerneldarrelltub

Books also available in… Kindle bookstores

Author's Note…

STARTING FROM…

RIGHT NOW!!! / THIS POINT ON!!!

NO MATTER WHO YOU ARE…

BELIEVE In YOURSELF…

Don't get caught up in what's going on around you…

Look at Your Situation/ Your Life… With a Clear Conscious… There is NO Rules To LIFE… YOU Chose Your Path… We all fall Down but WE Get Back UP… A Saint is a Sinner Who FELL DOWN but GOT BACK UP!!! And A WINNER is just a loser who didn't give up, and tried one more time…

S0, Start from Now…

Make Your Story, A Great One!!!

Control Your Mind…

It's Not Too Late… It's Never Too Late…

As long as you Are BREATHING…

You Can Do Anything!!!

(written by TUB)

...WHY I WRITE...

MY GOAL, as a WRITER/ AUTHOR, is to entertain the Reader, first of all... But My Ultimate Goal is to Help "Strengthen," The MIND OF MAN!!! I was going to say Black Man, but it is not technically about race OR even gender, so this applies for Women also... I feel the "SYSTEM" has done US All a "Dis-Service," from slavery and beyond... No, we are not Physically Slaves now, but they are got our "MINDS INSLAVED/ Our Minds Imprisoned..." They say that the most powerful prison is one when you don't even know that you're locked up... And They, (the system) are using, their Media Outlets, TV's, Music, and JAILS... To control US and keep their plan working...

They want us to keep thinking Barbaric... Like a Beast or Animal with no sense... They want us to keep killing each other, and falling victim to their systematic trap... I Think, this way of life, (systematic way) is far from the True way of Life... I Feel, Every Person Matters... That's why I refuse to CONFORM to anything, period...

They don't want us to be Peaceful, Conscious, Thinking human beings... So again, my Goal is to strengthen the Mind of Man- Kind, Especially the ones In Prison...

If I start there, then maybe we will have a better chance when we enter back into the systematic World, that they call Society...

When we return to "Society", They try to Paste the Stigma, of our Past on us… Once you commit a crime… And do the time/ the punishment… It's over!!! You CAN let it Go!!! We are not our Past, we are our Future… YOU CAN, Start Over… Fuck a "Revolving Door" You can leave Old Ways Behind You, and Move On!!! Don't Let Them Make You Out to be Worst then You Are…

Only You, can determine your Next Step… Do You Leave, the Crime/ Past Behind?? Do you Fall In-to The Systematic Trap, of Thinking, You CAN'T Change?? Or do you take a Stand, and Refuse to let your past be your future… Do you Put All Crime and Jail behind you, and Quest for a better future?? In the END… The Choice is Yours!!!

My Fellow MAN-KIND, START LOVING YOURSELF!!!

(Leave Jail Behind Us- FREEDOM is PRICELESS)

…WHY I WRITE…

By… GERNEL L. DARRELL

AKA

…TUB…

.

Printed in Great Britain
by Amazon

29653782R00090